"Armstrong and Mitchell have provided a comprehensive and concise overview of human resources with practical advice, tips, forms and check-lists. A must read for managers, small business owners, and individuals new to the HR profession."

—Cornelia Gamlem, SPHR, president of GEMS Group ltd. *www.gemsgroup-hr.com*

"Armstrong and Mitchell have given us an excellent primer to educate our newly hired or promoted people managers on the must-know elements of human resource management. From the perspective of both historical and emerging trends, they succinctly present a pragmatic and uncomplicated explanation of why and how these issues are essential to business success. Among the many nuggets they offer are numerous, practical and proven ways to safely say what needs to be said in employee conversations, interviews, and evaluations. Even this old dog learned some new tricks!"

—Gary Cluff, manager, Corporate Recruiting, The MITRE Corporation

"As a HR practitioner of 26 years, I strongly recommend this book to all HR professionals who want to bring added value, and who wants to become a significant strategic partner in their organization. This book is a must have for any HR professional's library."

—Ben Lastimado, ED, author, *Increasing Your HR Profession's Value— Make Them Want You For a Strategic Partner*

"If you want to know the core elements that any Human Resources professional should have in mind as they map their strategy and advise their organization, Sharon Armstrong's and Barbara Mitchell's work is a great source. And a strong manager should be keeping the points in *The Essential HR Handbook* front and center in their leadership of people! This is a great straight-forward resource for any desktop!"

—Naomi Morales, deputy vice president, Human Resources and Ad-ministration, PhRMA

"As promised in their introduction, the authors of *The Essential HR Handbook* have really made it all about the people. This is a handy reference for anyone trying to be an effective manager of people. If nothing else, be sure to read Chapter 12 and know the challenges for the future."

—Dr. Janet Stern Solomon, SPHR, professor of management, The George Washington University

"This book should become 'The Source' for professionals in Human Resources. It covers the essential considerations in the field in a well-written, authoritative and yet very readable style. If you are at all interested in the growing area of Human Resources, I strongly urge to read *The Essential HR Handbook* ."

—Henry P. Baer, former Chair of the Labor & Employment Law Practice, Skadden, Arps, Slate, Meagher & Flom LLP

"This concise handbook gets to the heart of human resource management by providing both practical guidance on essential HR activities and loads of useful samples, checklists and tools to help you do HR effectively and efficiently."

—Wendy Bliss, J.D., SPHR, author, *Employment Termination Source Book* and *Legal, Effective References: How to Give and Get Them*

"This book delivers on the promise made in the title. It offers great examples, useful templates, provocative questions and all the data that an HR person might want to have at their fingertips. It is easy to read and gets the reader to the main point quickly and easily. The appendix is superb. A must have for your shelf."

—Beverly Kaye, founder/CEO, Career Systems International, author of *Up Is Not the Only Way*

"Look no further than *The Essential HR Handbook* for the right advice to make the human resources function indispensable for the success of an organization. This book spells out practical approaches to the critical issues faced by leaders to effectively manage a fast-changing workforce. It is a must-read for all managers, not just HR professionals."

—Brad Taft, president, Taft Resource Group, Career and Workforce Development Consultants, coauthor of *Boom or Bust...Career Management Guide for Baby Boomers and Beyond*

"The title says it all. This handbook succinctly lays out the key principles and protections that every Human Resource professional needs to know and put in place. It's also a reference source that won't remain on your shelf for long."

—Francis T. Coleman, Esq., Williams Mullen

"*The Essential HR Handbook* is a superb compendium of human resources tools and techniques for HR and other professionals at all levels of organizations whether your company is large or small. This handbook provides extremely useful information on all facets of human resources and the sample documents (from applications through exit interviews) are especially helpful."

—Gail Hyland-Savage, COO, Michaelson, Connor & Boul

"I am confident that you will find *The Essential HR Handbook*, truly that—*essential* in establishing a significant HR infrastructure relevant to all organizations. Not only do the authors address the fundamentals necessary to support a growing organization, but they walk you through the importance and process of defining a strategic human resource plan. *The Essential HR Handbook* should be a part of every HR Tool Kit!"

—Kathy Albarado, SPHR, president of Helios HR, principal author of *Guide to HR Administration*

"HR is no longer trying to find a seat at the table. It has become an inherent part of every process and priority that enable an organization to achieve its goals. Armstrong and Mitchell have transformed years of meaningful experience into one practical, comprehensive work. *The Essential HR Handbook* is a nonpareil; it clearly specifies the core elements of human resource management that help lead organizations to sustained success."

—John G. Kitson, senior vice president, chief human resources officer, First Banks, Inc.

"Reading this extraordinary book, I asked myself how I have managed thus far without it? Not only is this a comprehensive guide to everything an HR professional needs to know, but the samples contained at the end of almost every chapter and the appendix loaded with every tool necessary, made me think I had hit the mother lode."

—Karen Bloom, principal of Bloom, Gross & Associates, Inc.

"Regardless of the business size or industry; profit, non-profit, or government, this book reinforces what I have learned throughout my HR career—without strategic alignment between HR & the business manager, the dynamics of organizational effectiveness are absent."

—D.J. Strauss, chief, branch of recruitment/training, DOL Office of Inspector General

The Essential
HR Handbook

A Quick and Handy Resource for
Any Manager or HR Professional

By Sharon Armstrong and
Barbara Mitchell

 C A R E E R   The Career Press, Inc.
P R E S S   Pompton Plains, NJ

THE ESSENTIAL HR HANDBOOK
EDITED AND TYPESET BY GINA TALUCCI
Cover design by Jeff Piasky
Printed in the U.S.A.

To order this title, please call toll-free 1-800-CAREER-1 (NJ and Canada: 201-848-0310) to order using VISA or MasterCard, or for further information on books from Career Press.

CAREER
PRESS

The Career Press, Inc., 220 West Parkway, Unit 12
Pompton Plains, NJ 07444
www.careerpress.com

Library of Congress Cataloging-in-Publication Data
Armstrong, Sharon, 1951–
    The essential HR handbook : a quick and handy resource for any manager or HR professional / by Sharon Armstrong and Barbara Mitchell.
        p. cm.
    ISBN 978-1-56414-990-9
    1. Personnel management. I. Mitchell, Barbara, 1943– II. Title.

HF5549.A89786 2008
658.3--dc22

2007052475

Dedication

This book is dedicated to my father, Charles B. Scott, who taught me the true meaning of perseverance.

—Sharon Scott Armstrong

This book is dedicated to my parents, Anne and Tom Mitchell—I wish they were here to celebrate this achievement with me.

—Barbara Mitchell

Acknowledgments

Most people understand that writing a book takes a village! There are many folks behind the scenes who helped us, so there are some thank yous due.

Three major heroes were Anne Goodfriend, who skillfully and kindly edited our thoughts and words while remaining calm throughout; Susan Devereaux, who put the final manuscript together in her typical (and wonderful) professional way; and Joyce Oliner, who went above and beyond with some important critiques and suggestions. Another significant and special friend was Mike Strand, who contributed two important chapters without breaking a sweat.

More shout-outs go to: Kathy Albarado, Marilyn Allen, Richard Armstrong, Kimberly Barton, Patti Bicknell, Jann Bradley, Irene Cardon, Ann Casso, Madelyne D'Angelo, Angela Dabbs, Amy Dufrane, Laurie Friedman, Saunji Fyffe, Cornelia Gamlem, Diane Gold, Allyn Gutauskas, Lisa Haneberg, Bob Hoffman, Anne Hull, Natalie Loeb, Joanne Lozar Glenn, Taren McCombs, Cheryl Mirabella, Naomi Morales,

Kerri Koss Morehart, Tom Morris, Julie Perez, Jane Pettit, Ane Powers, Michael Pye, Leah Rampy, Maggie Saponaro, Gail Hyland-Savage, Priscilla Vazquez, and Elaine Winfrey.

And finally, two special thanks to our literary agent, Marilyn Allen, for getting us started on this journey, and to our Career Press editor and formatter, Gina Talucci, for gently bringing the book to completion, thereby ending the journey.

To paraphrase the words of William Butler Yeats, "Think where man's glory most begins and ends, and say our glory was we had such friends."

Sharon Armstrong
Barbara Mitchell
Washington, D.C.

Contents

Introduction

*Leading today is like being a first-time parent—
you have to do the right thing long before you
fully understand the situation.*

—Warren Bennis, distinguished professor of business, and founding chairman of the Leadership Institute at the University of Southern California

In 14th-century England, masons, carpenters, leather workers, and other skilled craftsmen organized themselves into guilds, which they used to improve their work conditions.[1] These guilds were the beginning of unions.

John Ivancevich, in his book *Human Resource Management,* tells us that, with the Industrial Revolution of the late 18th and early 19th centuries, however, everything changed: divisions of labor, wages and hours, working conditions, and more. A new character in the workplace replaced the owner: the boss.[2] He focused on getting the job done fast and done right.

Conflict grew between bosses and employees, and as businesses expanded they established new departments to deal with issues in the workplace. During the 1930s and 1940s, personnel departments began appearing to address hiring, firing, and the conflicts that occurred in between.

Around this time, personnel managers focused on employees and their well being, sharing their observations and suggestions with management to improve employees' working lives.

Business guru Peter Drucker, the father of modern management and a prolific author, wrote that the role of personnel staff was "partly a file clerk's job, partly a housekeeping job, partly a social worker's job, and partly firefighting, heading off union trouble."[3]

Gone are the days (we hope) when managers wanted only that the work be done right and fast—without regard to the "human resources," the workers. Both good managers and HR professionals need to understand their organizations' employees and, on their behalf, create a workplace that helps them do their best work.

Some organizations have renamed their personnel/human resources units "People" or "Human Capital" departments to emphasize the importance of their paramount resource. They know that, without good people management, nothing else matters.

Today, leaders of successful organizations understand the importance of good human resources principles and practices for maintaining a healthy business: They expect their managers to integrate good human resources management into their day-to-day work.

In fact, in order to survive in today's increasingly challenging world of work, managers have to be lifelong learners. They have to be open to not only learning new things, but also to incorporating those things in their everyday approach to work. These two behaviors are among the most critical for honing managerial skills.

That sounds simple, but we know that human resources is a complex field. HR tools and techniques draw on a wide and growing body of knowledge and requirements. The challenge for managers is to stay informed of the field's best practices. What does "human resources" mean today? It is the process of acquiring, training, appraising, and compensating employees while attending to their concerns about labor relations, health and safety, and fairness.[4]

This book covers these critical functions, working conditions, and the management actions—major or minor—that support them. It provides practical information, tools, and techniques to help managers and HR professionals excel.

When Joe Gibbs, former coach of the NFL's Washington Redskins and three-time NASCAR champion, was asked to describe the differences between professional football and professional car racing, he replied, "There is none; it's all about the people."[5]

Now that's a worthy mantra for managers and HR professionals: It's all about the people.

Chapter 1
Strategic Planning and Mission Statements

Strategy connects the purpose and values of your organization with those of its customers and other external shareholders.

—Tony Manning, *Making Sense of Strategy*

If you don't know where you're going, how will you know when you get there? That's why every organization needs a statement of its purpose or mission, and a strategy for planning its future.

Organizational strategy

Managers are responsible for allocating resources to achieve their organization's stated goals, and this is where organizational strategy comes into play. Successful management of resources depends on effective planning. Managers need to set the organizations' strategic direction and develop a plan to implement the strategy.

That plan defines the organization's path into the future, and implementing it involves making decisions about the allocation of resources to reach the goals.

Organizational resources include intellectual capital, products, and financial capital, but the most important resource of all is human capital—the people who make it all happen. And because most organizations spend the largest percentage of their dollars on their labor force, firms that align their people strategies with their organizational ones are the most successful.

If you don't know where you're going, how will you know when you get there? It all starts with deciding what the organization wants to achieve throughout a reasonable period of time. In the past, standard business practice was to plan for long periods, such as five, 10, or 20 years—but, in today's volatile business climate, most organizations plan for shorter periods such as one, three, or at most five years.

For your organization to remain competitive, it is essential to revisit your strategic plan frequently, and explore the business climate in your organization's field to understand changes that may affect your company and its strategy. Strategy development involves evaluating the organization's current business situation and determining where it wants to go in the future. Managing strategy is never "cast in concrete"—it is a continuous, recurring process.

Developing a strategic plan

The most enlightened organizations include human resources (HR) in the development of the strategic plan, so that the human resources plan can link directly to the strategic plan (discussed later in this chapter).

The typical approach to strategic planning is a three-step process:
1. Establish why the organization exists, its mission.

2. Define what you want the organization's near future to be.

3. Establish what needs to be done—and what needs to be done differently—to reach the stated objectives.

Crafting a mission statement

Organizational strategy consists of concisely, clearly, and carefully communicating to everyone in the organization where the company is headed, which is the first step in creating a mission statement. This document describes what the organization is today, and what it values, in succinct and measurable terms.

See the end of this chapter for an example: the mission statement of the grocery-store chain Wegmans—a highly successful organization consistently listed on *Fortune* magazine's annual list of 100 Best Companies to Work For in America.

The Wegmans declaration clearly states what the company values in its employees and articulates its primary goal: meeting the needs of its employees and exceeding the needs of its customers.

Elements of a Mission Statement

Mission statements should be succinct and easy for employees, customers, and the general public to understand. Some of the elements to consider as you craft a mission statement include your organization's:

✓ *Desired image in the marketplace.*

✓ *Target market for products or services.*

✓ *Products or services (described).*

✓ *Local, national, or global reach—where your clients are located.*

A place where you can begin to develop a strategic plan is to ask a series of questions that will produce the information you need to take the next step in defining the organization's future direction. *Here are some sample questions:*

✓ What are your plans for growth?

✓ What is your ethics statement?

✓ What challenges are you facing today?

✓ What are your competitors doing that you aren't doing?

✓ What sets you apart from the competition?

✓ What changes have occurred in your industry or service area?

✓ How has globalization affected your organization?

✓ Have your competitors entered the global market?

✓ Are there opportunities outside your current market to consider?

✓ Is your technology up-to-date?

✓ What affect has technology had on your customers, members, or employees?

✓ Have your customers' or members' expectations changed?

✓ What are you doing to retain any competitive advantage you have?

✓ What are your distinctive, competitive strengths, and how does the plan build on them?

✓ How will changes in your strategy affect your employees?

✓ Do you have the people resources you need to reach your desired goals?

✓ What effect will changing demographics have on your strategy?

✓ What legal or regulatory changes do you anticipate that may affect your strategy?

✓ How and why is this plan different from the previous one? Were all your elements completed? If not, why? How could you have prevented that?

✓ How different is your strategy from those of your competitors, and why? Is that good or bad? What do you know about your competitors' strategies?

✓ How accurate have your past budgets and projections been? What could have made them more accurate?

✓ Who will measure the outcomes of the strategy, with what tools? How often will you monitor progress?

After answering these questions, you can decide how the organization will capitalize on its strengths, eliminate or minimize its weaknesses, exploit opportunities, and defend against threats.

Putting your plan in motion

If the organization sets out a good strategic direction and sets goals and measurements to ensure the goals are met, it can envision its future.

But after the vision is set forth, nothing will happen without an implementation strategy. This is where responsibilities are determined and accountabilities defined. A time line should be created, and milestone reviews should be scheduled, so that the strategic plan is constantly in front of the leadership and discussed at staff meetings. The time line should be reviewed and updated in order to keep it as current as possible.

Communicating the plan

Once the strategic plan is developed and easily understood, it is extremely important to share it with the employees. This can be in writing, sent as an e-mail from the leader of the organization, or communicated in person at an "all staff" meeting. How the message gets out isn't nearly as important as the fact that it is communicated. Employees need to know where their organization is headed, and how the work they do fits into the plan.

Linking HR planning to the strategic plan

Organizations that link the overall strategic plan to their plans for finding and keeping employees tend to be the most successful in today's competitive marketplace. After an organization's strategic plan is in place, it is important to identify the roles the human resources department will play in achieving the organization's goals.

Once the strategic areas that will affect employees are identified, the planners need to determine whether the organization lacks any resources that will prevent HR from fully participating. For example, the organization may not have developed a robust benefits package yet, inhibiting its ability to compete for the talent it needs.

It is at this point in the process that HR issues—a critical element in the strategic plan—really come into play. Organizations that involve HR in the strategic planning process soon learn that issues about people have an affect on nearly every organizational activity.

For example, if the plan calls for building a new manufacturing facility in South America, it is probably HR that will need to research labor markets and union activity in different countries, look at compensation plans, investigate the process for obtaining work permits and visas for U.S. nationals, research applicable benefit plans, and gather data on whether the organization's current health plan covers workers out of the country.

If growth is projected in the strategic plan, HR should consider creating a workforce plan. This involves looking at the current workforce in depth and asking questions such as:

✓ What are the strengths and areas of concern with the current workforce?

✓ Who is eligible to retire?

✓ Are there current employees with performance issues?

✓ Does the projected growth mean additional workers will be needed?

✓ What skills and abilities—technical, administrative, managerial, and leadership—are needed to accomplish the work?

✓ Are there gaps in the current skills of the workforce, and what will be required to achieve the new strategic direction?

Once these questions are answered, HR can begin to address how gaps can be filled. For example, if the strategy involves increasing the number of technical employees in a particular department, some solutions might be:

✓ Hiring new employees.

✓ Training existing employees.

✓ Transfering employees from another location.

✓ Doing all three.

If the choice is to hire new employees, the organization needs to plan how to assimilate them into the workplace culture and ensure a smooth transition.

Linking HR and the organization

A typical criticism of HR professionals is that they do not understand the businesses in which they work. They are too focused on their own area of the business, say critics, and don't always take the time to understand marketing, finance, and business operations.

Although HR is increasingly complex, it is not a stand-alone function. For HR professionals to be true business partners, they must learn as much as possible about the operation of their organizations' business. Studying business plans, strategic plans, annual reports, and other written documents is one of the best ways to do this; so is networking with others in the organization.

Some successful HR people say that when they join a new firm, they make a list of people they want to meet, then start asking them to lunch or coffee. While out of the office, they ask a series of questions about their colleagues' function in the organization. Most people enjoy sharing their expertise, and, if you approach these conversations properly and respect colleagues' busy schedules, this strategy can be very effective. Possible questions can include:

✓ How long have you been with the XYZ Company?

✓ What about this organization attracted you to it?

✓ What has been your greatest challenge at XYZ?

✓ What has been your greatest success?

✓ What keeps you up at night?

✓ How does your department fit into the company's overall mission?

✓ How can the HR function help you and your staff achieve your goals?

✓ What has XYZ's HR done well in the past, and where can it improve?

✓ Can you recommend books or other reference material so that I can learn more about what you do as [position]?

✓ Are there organizations you recommend I join to network with people in this field?

✓ Is there anything else you can tell me that will help me be the best possible business partner for you and your department?

These conversations should be dialogues, not interviews, and as informal as possible. Ideally, you will be asked to share your background and goals as well.

It is critical for people in the HR function, whether they are full-time HR professionals or managers who bear HR responsibilities, to learn the language of the organization and participate in discussions about overall strategy. This may take some time to develop, but it is extremely important in order to link the people issues to the rest of the corporate strategy.

HR people need access to information about changes in employment laws and government regulations. They also need access to others in the HR field so they can share "best practices" or ask for help with a particular problem. The Society for Human Resource Management (SHRM) provides a wealth of learning opportunities as well as resources on its Website at *www.shrm.org*. The organization also has local chapters, most of which meet monthly for professional development programs and networking.

Main message for managers

Organizations need to set a strategic direction to know where they are headed and how they are going to get there. HR managers, along with amanagers of other departments, should be key players in defining the strategic plan. Once the plan is developed, attention should be paid to developing an HR plan that links to and supports the organization's strategic plan—because, without the right people in the right positions, odds are the strategic goals won't be met.

Anyone who has responsibility for HR in an organization needs to understand the business the company is in and be able to speak the language of that business.

Sample mission statements

Used with permission of each organization.

Wegmans, grocery store chain—What We Believe[1]

At Wegmans, we believe that good people, working toward a common goal, can accomplish anything they set out to do.

In this spirit, we set our goal to be the very best at serving the needs of our customers. Every action we take should be made with this in mind.

We also believe that we can achieve our goal only if we fulfill the needs of our own people.

To our customers and our people we pledge continuous improvement, and we make the commitment, "Every day you get our best."

The National Council of La Raza (NCLR), the largest national Hispanic civil rights and advocacy organization in the United States, works to improve opportunities for Hispanic Americans. Through its network of nearly 300 affiliated community-based organizations (CBOs), NCLR reaches millions of Hispanics each year in 41 states, Puerto Rico, and the District of Columbia. To achieve its mission, NCLR conducts applied research, policy analysis, and advocacy, providing a Latino perspective in five key areas—assets/investments, civil rights/immigration, education, employment and economic status, and health. In addition, it provides capacity-building assistance to its affiliates who work at the state and local level to advance opportunities for individuals and families. Founded in 1968, NCLR is a private, nonprofit, nonpartisan, tax-exempt organization headquartered in Washington, D.C. NCLR serves all Hispanic subgroups in all regions of the country and has operations in Atlanta, Chicago, Los Angeles, New York, Phoenix, Sacramento, San Antonio, and Puerto Rico.

Michaelson, Connor & Boul. We exist to be a real estate services corporation that is profitable through continued growth and diversity. We are technology driven, efficient, and results-oriented, but flexible to exceed our clients' needs. Integrity is of utmost importance.

The National Association of Federal Credit Unions is a direct membership association committed to advancing the credit union community through its relentless focus on membership value in representing, assisting, educating, and informing its member credit unions and their key audiences.

As a trusted advisor, **Helios HR** provides its clients a competitive advantage: the creation of a culture that attracts, retains, and engages an exceptional workforce.

The mission of the **Optical Society of America** (OSA) is to promote the generation, application, and archiving of knowledge in optics and photonics and to disseminate this knowledge worldwide. The purposes of the Society are scientific, technical, and educational. Founded in 1916, OSA brings together optics and photonics scientists, engineers, educators, technicians, and business leaders. OSA is dedicated to providing its members and the scientific community with educational resources that support technical and professional development. OSA publications, events, and services help to advance the science of light by addressing the ongoing need for shared knowledge and innovation. The Society's commitment to excellence and long-term learning is the driving force behind all its initiatives.

PhRMA's mission is winning advocacy for public policies that encourage the discovery of life-saving and life-enhancing new medicines for patients by biopharmaceutical research companies. To accomplish this mission, PhRMA (Pharmaceutical Research and

Manufacturers of America) is dedicated to achieving in Washington, D.C., the states, and the world:

✓ Broad patient access to safe and effective medicines through a free market, without price controls.

✓ Strong intellectual property incentives.

✓ Transparent, efficient regulation and a free flow of information to patients.

Farmington Country Club is a traditional, family-oriented private club with a proud history, rich traditions, and commitment to the customs of Southern hospitality and gracious living. As the premier, full-service private club in central Virginia, Farmington shall provide excellent facilities, programs, and services to serve the social, athletic, and recreational needs of its members, their families, and their guests.

NeighborWorks® America creates opportunities for people to live in affordable homes, improve their lives, and strengthen their communities.

The White Hawk Group LLC is dedicated to providing professional, high quality guidance and related services to individuals and organizations in the process of change and/or transition. In the delivery of career management and leadership development coaching and training, WHG is committed to assisting clients understand and communicate current realities; assess strengths and potential obstacles to success; clarify goals; and develop and implement effective plans for goal attainment.

Chapter 2
Optimal Staffing

The ultimate throttle on growth for any company is...the ability to get and keep enough of the right people.

—Jim Collins, *Good to Great*

The hiring process is critical to the success of your company. Done well, it can build a hard-working, loyal staff and help grow your business; done poorly, it can increase turnover and stunt your staff.

Finding applicants

It used to be simple: You ran an ad in the newspaper, and applicants either mailed in a résumé or applied in person. Now, applicants also use your company's Website or one of the many online job sites—from general ones such as *www.monster.com*

or *www.careerbuilder.com*, to industry-specific ones such as *www.journalismjobs.com*. To stay competitive and attract applicants, you may also need to participate in job fairs, recruit at local colleges or trade schools, run ads on the radio, or hold open houses at your workplace.

When you advertise or post a position, it is important to stress the benefits of working for your organization. That is what applicants want to know ("What's in it for me?"). Another critical element is setting your company apart from all the others that are hiring for the same type of position: What can you tell job seekers that will excite them enough to contact your organization? Of course include the job requirements and what is expected of the chosen applicant, state the date by which applications must be received, and always provide multiple ways for applicants to contact your organization, including online applications, a fax number, and a street address to send a paper application. Direct applicants to your firm's Website to learn more about the company.

One of the best and the most cost-effective sources for applicants is an employee referral program. It produces high-quality applicants (because your current employees won't want a bad referral to reflect on them personally) and lets you gauge employee morale (because employees won't refer others if they are not happy in their jobs).

Employee referral programs can range from a simple e-mail asking all employees to refer friends, to contests with cash awards or prizes for employees whose referrals are hired. If you use a recruitment agency, it can design a program to meet your needs.

Keeping in touch with former employees you'd like to hire again is another excellent strategy. Some of the world's largest and most successful companies bring such "boomerangs" back by letting talented employees who leave know that they will be welcome to return. Top companies stay in touch with such employees and keep them connected to the organization by sending them announcements of new clients or awards. Then, when the time is right, they invite them back. When boomerangs return, they come with new skill sets and, typically, renewed commitment to the organization.

Reference Checking Form

Applicant:
Date:
Reference provided by: [name]
Organization:
Dates of employment:
Title:
General responsibilities:
Relationship to applicant:

We are considering hiring [name] for [position] in [organization]. How well do you think he [or she] will do in that position?

Please comment on the overall quality of the applicant's work at your organization.

Please discuss how the applicant worked with others in your organization.

Why did [name] leave your organization?

Is he [or she] eligible for rehire?

Is there anything else you'd like to share about [name] that will help us make a good decision?

Thank you for your time and comments.

(Note: Many organizations require that all requests for employment information be directed to the HR department or to a designated individual. Generally, the only information those companies release is factual, such as date of hire, title, or length of service. Subjective information—such as comments on performance or reasons for a former employee's termination—is not shared.)

Reviewing resumes

When the resumes start pouring in, be prepared with a plan for determining whom to interview. First, have a thorough understanding of the position: Identify specifically what you want the new employee to do and the results you want him or her to achieve. Determine which elements of performance or behavior—such as teamwork, reliability, and tolerance—are critical in this job, and what skills, abilities, and knowledge the successful applicant must have. If your list of requirements is long, prioritize them.

As you review résumés, here are some red flags to watch out for:

✓   No dates for previous jobs.

✓   Gaps in employment.

✓   Job-hopping with decreasing responsibilities.

✓   Accomplishments listed but not tied to a particular position.

When you've narrowed down the stack of résumés, you may want to do a quick screening interview by phone to ask very specific questions before setting up a face-to-face interview. Focus your screening interview on determining whether the applicant has the basic skills for the position and is within your salary range. To save everyone's time, let the job seeker know the range at the beginning of the call, and ask whether the interview should continue. It is among the first things that applicants want to know, yet they're very reluctant to specify their most recent salary or their desired range, for fear they'll limit themselves or be dismissed as over- or under-qualified. Be sensitive to this. Here is a sample telephone screening form:

Telephone Screen Form

Position: _____
Date:_____

Candidate's name:_____

Interviewer:_____

Background and education:

Does not meet requirements
Meets minimum requirements
Exceeds requirements

Technical skills:

Does not meet requirements
Meets minimum requirements
Exceeds requirements

Interpersonal and communication skills:

Does not meet requirements
Meets minimum requirements
Exceeds requirements

Salary requirements:

Below position range
Within position range
Exceeds position range

Recommendation:

Reject candidate   Rejection letter sent

Schedule in-person interview   Interview scheduled

Hold résumé/application for future opening

Interviewing applicants

Once you set up an interview, find a private place to conduct it where you won't be interrupted. That's just common courtesy. It is extremely important to treat applicants courteously so they feel good about the interview experience and your organization—even if they aren't selected for the position. Try to create goodwill for your company regardless of the outcome.

Most of us have made the mistake of hiring someone who either lacked the necessary skills or didn't fit the organization's culture. But we can reduce the risk of doing that with behavioral interviewing, a systematic, analytical, and objective technique.

A behavioral interview is carefully planned and based on the job and its outcomes, according to the principle that past performance is the best indicator of future behavior. Specifically, it assumes that the way a job applicant has used his or her skills in the past will predict how he or she will use them in a new job. Managers should design questions to draw out candidates' stories of real-life experiences that illustrate their ability to perform the essential functions, reach the applicable goals, and excel in the job.

Good behavioral interview questions allow you to draw out the candidate's strengths, areas for development, and suitability for your open position. They also will help you determine whether the applicant will fit into your work environment.

Those good questions will often start with:

✓ Tell me about a time....

✓ Give me an example of when....

✓ Walk me through....

✓ Describe for me....

For instance, if the person you hire must be *flexible*, consider asking, "Give me an example of a time when priorities were shifted. How did you react?" Is *quality of work* important? "Tell me about a time when your boss was not satisfied with an assignment you completed."

Make sure that interview questions do not solicit information that employers are legally barred from considering in the hiring process, such as age, gender, religion, race, color, national origin, and/or disability. (See Chapter 9.)

Sample behavioral-interview questions

Ability to accept constructive criticism

✓ Describe a time when your work on an idea of yours was criticized.

Ability to work under pressure

✓ Describe a situation in which you were required to work under pressure and how you reacted.

✓ Describe a time when you were given a job or assignment for which you had no prior training. How did you learn to do it?

Accomplishments

✓ Describe your three greatest accomplishments on the job.

✓ What was the most satisfying accomplishment in your last job? What made it so satisfying?

✓ Give an example of a time when you set a goal and met or achieved it.

✓ Describe a time when you set your sights too high.

✓ What are some obstacles that you have had to overcome to get where you are today? How did you handle them?

Challenging situations

✓ Describe a situation when you faced a challenge and how you met it.

Communication skills

✓ Talk about a time when you had to communicate verbally to get an important point across, and tell me how you did it.

✓ Did you ever have an experience at work in which you had to speak up and tell other people what you thought or felt? What was the outcome?

✓ Give an example of a time when you were able to communicate successfully with another person who might not have liked you personally.

✓ Have you ever made a presentation? When? Why? What was the outcome?

✓ Describe the most significant document, report, or presentation you have created.

✓ Have you ever had to "sell" an idea to your colleagues, team, or group? How did you do it? Did they "buy" it?

✓ Describe an instance when you had to think on your feet to extricate yourself from a difficult situation.

Conflict management

✓ What is your typical way of dealing with conflict? Give an example. Talk about a time when you had to manage a conflict or dispute among staff who reported to you or members of a team.

✓ Describe a time when you worked with others who did not work well together. How did you deal with that?

Coping skills

✓ Describe a time when you were faced with problems or stresses at work and how you coped with them.

✓ Talk about a high-stress situation when you needed to keep a positive attitude. What happened?

✓ When you find yourself frustrated by a roadblock, what do you do? Give an example.

Creativity

✓ Describe your most creative work-related project.

Customer service

✓ Give an example of a time when you used your customer philosophy to deal with a problem.

Dealing with difficult people

✓ Talk about a time in the past year when you had to deal with a difficult team member, and describe what you did.

✓ Think about a difficult boss or colleague and what made him or her that way. How did you interact with this person?

✓ Describe your worst-ever customer or co-worker and how you dealt with him or her.

Decision-making

✓ What is the riskiest job-related decision you've ever made?

✓ Describe a difficult decision you've made in the past year.

✓ Give an example of a time when you had to make a decision relatively quickly.

or:

✓ Give an example of a time when you had to make a split-second decision.

✓ Describe an unpopular decision you were forced to make.

✓ Have you ever had to refrain from speaking or making a decision because you did not have enough information? What happened? What did you learn from this experience?

✓ Describe a decision you made within the past year that you're very proud of.

Delegating

✓ Give an example of an instance in which you delegated a project effectively.

✓ Talk about a time when you were given a vague assignment yet completed it successfully. What was the situation? What, specifically, did you do? What was the result?

Initiative
- ✓ When and how have you shown initiative?
- ✓ Give an example of a time when you had to go above and beyond the call of duty to get a job done.
- ✓ Have you ever performed duties beyond the scope of your job description? How did you handle this?
- ✓ Have you worked on a difficult assignment with few or no resources? What did you do, and what was the result?

Leadership
- ✓ One leadership skill is the ability to accommodate different views in the workplace, regardless of what they are. What have you done to foster a wide number of views in your work environment?
- ✓ What personal qualities define you as a leader? Describe a situation when these qualities helped you lead others.
- ✓ Give an example of when you demonstrated good leadership.
- ✓ What is the toughest group from which you've had to get cooperation?
- ✓ Have you ever had difficulty getting others to accept your ideas? What was your approach? Did it work?
- ✓ Describe a situation in which you had to change your leadership style to have the desired impact.

Motivation
- ✓ What's important to you in a job?
- ✓ Why does this position interest you? What attracts you to our organization?

or:

- ✓ What have you learned about our organization?
- ✓ How do you motivate people? Give a specific example of something you did that helped build others' enthusiasm.

✓ How have you motivated yourself to complete an assignment or task you did not want to do?

✓ Describe techniques you've used to recognize or reward staff performance.

✓ Talk about a time when you led a group to achieve a goal.

Persistence

✓ When has your persistence had the biggest payoff?

✓ Give an example of an important goal and describe your progress in reaching it.

Persuasion

✓ Summarize a situation where you persuaded others to take action or to see your point of view.

or:

✓ Describe a time when you used facts and reason to persuade someone to take action.

Planning

✓ Talk about a complex assignment you planned and executed. How did you do it?

Problem-solving

✓ Describe a major problem you faced and how you dealt with it.

or:

✓ Describe a situation in which you solved a problem by combining different perspectives or approaches.

or:

✓ Think about a complex project or assignment you received. What approach did you take to complete it?

✓ Describe an instance when you, or a group you were in, were in danger of missing a deadline. What did you do?

✓ Give an example of how you used your fact-finding skills to get information you needed to solve a problem;

how did you analyze the information and reach a decision?

✓ What do you do when your priorities don't match those of your colleagues?

✓ Describe a specific instance when you used good judgment and logic in solving a problem.

✓ Think of a time when members of your group disagreed but you had to achieve consensus. What was your approach? What was the outcome?

✓ Did you ever have to seek out "experts" in your organization to understand something? How did you do it? What were the results?

✓ How do you approach an unfamiliar task? Give an example.

Quick study

✓ Describe a situation when you had to learn something new in a very short time. How did you do it?

Process improvement

✓ Describe a couple of specific examples of your making something better or improving a service or product. How did you do it?

✓ Talk about an improvement you wanted to make in a process and the steps you took to do so.

✓ Have you ever recognized a problem before your boss or co-workers did? What did you do?

✓ Describe presenting a new idea to your supervisor. What was the result?

Supervision

✓ How many people have you supervised? If we talked to them, what three things would they say about your managerial style?

✓ What's the hardest part of managing people?

✓ Describe a situation in which a staff member was not performing to your expectations and how you handled it.

Teamwork

✓ How do you turn people who work for you into a team? What has worked? What hasn't? Give specific examples.

✓ Describe a time when you worked with someone who did things very differently from how you did them. How did you get the job done?

✓ What did you do in your last job to contribute toward an environment of teamwork? Be specific.

But questions alone—even great ones—do not make an interview good! What does? The interviewer's capacity for listening effectively, avoiding quick judgments, accepting silences, and remaining objective.

Tom Morris of Morris Associates, Inc., reminds us:

Sometimes you have to guide the interviewee through answering behavior-based questions, since they haven't been trained how to respond to them. One way to do this is to ask an open-ended behavioral question at the outset, and tell them how to respond: "[Name], could you tell me about something you did in your most recent position that you were particularly proud of? Tell me the challenge you were faced with and what steps you took … how you did it, and what the end result was."

As they give their example, guide them back through the steps above so they learn the process while answering so they know how to frame their responses to other behavior-based questions you will ask.

You've already established your standards for evaluating the candidates; make sure your evaluation of them is an objective tool.

Sample Applicant Evaluation Form

Applicant's name:_____
Interviewer:_____
Position:_____
Date:_____

Technical skills	Excellent			Poor	
[Criterion]	5	4	3	2	1
[Criterion]	5	4	3	2	1
[Criterion]	5	4	3	2	1

Comments:

Education	Excellent			Poor	
[Criterion]	5	4	3	2	1
[Criterion]	5	4	3	2	1
[Criterion]	5	4	3	2	1

Comments:

Work habits	Excellent			Poor	
[Criterion]	5	4	3	2	1
[Criterion]	5	4	3	2	1
[Criterion]	5	4	3	2	1

Comments:

Interpersonal skills	Excellent			Poor	
[Criterion]	5	4	3	2	1
[Criterion]	5	4	3	2	1
[Criterion]	5	4	3	2	1

Comments

Here's a suggested format for your interviews:

✓ Set the tone. Make the candidate feel comfortable and establish rapport.

✓ Let the candidate know you will be asking questions about his or her workplace behavior and taking notes, and that he or she will have time to ask questions after you've completed yours.

✓ Ask your prepared behavioral interview questions. Politely return to the original question if the candidate's answer is evasive. If the response is incomplete, ask follow-up questions.

✓ Describe the position and the company. (Don't describe the position in detail before this point, because a seasoned interviewee will just parrot your words to show you that he or she is the ideal candidate.)

✓ Respond to the candidate's questions.

✓ Explain the next step in the process and the time line for the employer's decision. Never give an applicant reason to believe that he or she is either a shoo-in or already rejected.

✓ Close the interview by asking, "Is there anything else you think we should know that we haven't already discussed?"

✓ Thank the applicant for his or her time—and remember, every applicant is a potential customer or member.

Some organizations rely on pre-employment testing to evaluate applicants' skills and abilities. Before you conduct any test, check with your firm's labor attorney to ensure that every question is work-related and non-discriminatory.

Main message for managers

Attracting and retaining skilled staff is one of your most important strategic priorities.

To make a successful hire, have a clear understanding of the job, prepare targeted behavioral interview questions, and be a good listener. Your job during the interview is to objectively assess the applicant by describing the job and the work environment positively and honestly, creating goodwill for your company—whether the applicant is hired or not.

Once a candidate is hired, it's time to celebrate, orient, and assimilate the new staff member!

Chapter 3
Orientation and Onboarding

Every orientation presupposes a disorientation.
—Hans Magnus Enzensberger, German author
and poet

Employees are critical resources. The smart manager realizes how important it is to help them get started on the right foot.

Orientation

The first step in facilitating a smooth transition to your workplace is an effective orientation. It's important to give new employees what they need in order to do what you hired them to do. And they should do it in a way that complements your workplace culture.

An article in *Training and Development* magazine, "Successful Orientation Programs," says a successful orientation should accomplish several objectives.

A critical one is that the new employee should understand the organization, in both a broad sense (its past and present, its culture, and its vision for the future) and a detailed sense (policies, procedures, and other key facts).[1]

Because that's a lot to cover, many organizations divide the material into different learning modules and present them throughout a period of time. Some organizations also have key staff members participate to thoroughly explain aspects of their operations—and their important connections with other areas of the firm—to new employees.

Some managers prefer to conduct their own orientations after the employee has completed one coordinated by the HR department. This reinforces what's important in the department.

Other managers collaborate with the HR department to make sure that the orientation covers topics necessary for new hires to succeed.

Sample New Employee Orientation Schedule

Day 1, [Date]

Time	Subject
9:00–9:15 a.m.	**Initial check-in with supervisor**

9:15–9:30 a.m.   **Computer and telephone systems**
Logging in/out, passwords, e-mail, viruses, home/resource directories. Review files.

10:00 a.m.–Noon **Review of HR policies and employee benefits** (with director of human resources) Review forms for employment and benefits. Review informational items in the New Employee packet.Review of HR policies and procedures.Tour of offices and introduction to staff.

3:00 p.m. Meet the President/CEO

Day 2, [Date]
Time
10:00–10:30 a.m. Mailroom (with Office Services clerk) Mail, in/out boxes. Publications routing, sign-up sheet. Routing card/reading files/boxes for filing. Couriers/FedEx/UPS. Copiers/fax machines/speed-dial numbers. Office supplies.

2:00–3:00 p.m. Office procedures and building facilities (with Associate Director for Administration) Review Office Procedures Manual.All-staff meetings. Travel.Building issues: problems/repairs. Visitors. Reception area. Parking. Emergency procedures. Inclement weather.

Courtesy of Irene Cardon, director of Human Resources and Administration, National Association of Federal Credit Unions, Arlington, Virginia.

Bringing new employees on board

Similar to building a successful marriage, incorporating new hires into an organization—or "onboarding"—requires developing a mutually satisfying relationship. As companies compete for talent, they need to adopt long-term strategies to integrate and retain new employees. The following are four opportunities to do so from Laurie Friedman of Strategic Business Consulting.

The first impression

Recruitment brings potential new hires to your door, but how well your organization manages the interview process affects whether an applicant takes the job. It also sets the stage for his or her long-term impressions of your organization. The first impression creates a lasting impression.

Research suggests that new employees decide within the first 30 days whether or not they feel welcome in the workplace. To retain and engage them, the company needs to leverage the enthusiasm, energy, and excitement they bring to the staff. Using strategies such as meet-and-greets, door banners, or bulletin-board notes to introduce new colleagues lets them know you're glad they're here.

Orientation programming

Typically, onboarding programs comprise a one- or two-day orientation that highlights the company mission, policies, and procedures—and explains how to use the organization's different information systems.

This approach can work if it gives new hires the information they need to succeed in the job. Too often, though, orientation programs focus on administrative details and lack a clear statement of how the job contributes to the company's overall success. The key is to articulate your company's vision, mission, and values in words and actions. Make sure your organization's onboarding goals are aligned with its business objectives in the orientation.

Beyond orientation, however, recruiting, retaining, and developing top talent requires more than a well-designed talent-management program. Organizations need to shift focus from their one- or two-day orientations by HR staff to a process that involves the entire staff. Top leaders must buy into and support the effort, with HR helping to ensure that executives across the organization understand and are committed to the program, so that the company vision and mission are adequately translated, and its hiring managers support the onboarding process.

To succeed in their jobs, new employees need to be drawn into the team and the organizational family. When new hires don't succeed, it's often because they're not a "good fit" within the culture of the workplace. Research by Recruitment Solutions shows that 47 percent of employee turnover occurs in the first 90 days.

Metrics

You can't manage what you don't measure. Some key aspects to quantify are turnover, how long it takes for new hires to become productive, and employee satisfaction. Keeping track of measures such as this provide support for developing and improving strategic onboarding programs. It's expensive to find and train new employees (some estimates say as much as half their first-year salary).

Putting it all together

Developing a strategic, formal approach to onboarding will lead to greater employee retention and engagement. If your organization suffers from a one-size-fits-all orientation approach, and if you believe that talent is walking out your door, it makes business sense to review and strengthen your new-hire processes.

Building onboarding procedures that span the employee's career are adaptable and flexible to meet changing needs, and include company-wide leadership will keep your workforce strong.

Main message for managers

It's important to acclimate new employees to the organization and its operational culture. Plan a program that will effectively welcome and engage the new employee. Make sure it's more than a rundown of administrative details—it needs to involve the entire staff and include specific measures to determine its effectiveness. And don't forget: the first impression creates a lasting impression!

Chapter 4
Training and Development

Ancora imparo (I am still learning).
　　—Michelangelo, sculptor, architect, painter, and
poet

Employees need a workplace where they can develop their professional and interpersonal skills.

Adult learning theory

Let's start with the basics. Lisa Haneberg, author of the forthcoming *10 Steps to Be a Successful Manager: Facilitator's Guide,* says:

> Managers are people, adults for the most part, so it would make sense that we could apply the basic assumptions of adult learning to the art and practice of training managers, right? As a reminder, here are some

of the basic beliefs about how adults learn and how trainers should use this information:

✓ Adult learners need to feel that the new information and skills directly link to and benefit their goals. They need to be enrolled with their hearts and minds to be engaged in the learning.

✓ Adult learners respond well to real-world examples and applications. Be sure to have conversations with trainees about how the principles and practices relate to their realities.

✓ Adult learners resist and repel being forced to attend trainings. They want to come up with the ideas for learning and development on their own or have a list of options from which to choose. Trainers should refrain from prescribing training or development. Instead, have open conversations with trainees and ask questions that allow them to discover and determine their development options.

✓ Adult learners may be defensive or feel attacked when training is recommended to them. Put your trainees in control, asking them to define their goals and the information or skills that would most help them reach their goals.

✓ Adult learners are invested in their careers and successes. They may be reluctant to share their mistakes or weaknesses. Help trainees find the right learning environments and redefine success such that open discussions and learning evoke less fear and insecurity.

✓ Adult learners own their progress and welcome clear feedback along the way. Help trainees determine how well their development is progressing and encourage them to begin applying new skills right away.

✓ Adult learners come to training or development sessions with years of previous experiences, opinions, and mind-sets. Ensure that they have the opportunity to share, acknowledge, and move beyond their biases. Concepts and practices that run counter to their usual ways of being will be accepted and applied slowly. Trainers should understand and allow time for this transition to occur.

✓ Adult learners cannot be forced to learn; they must be coachable, and this is their choice. Help facilitate their progress through open and candid conversations focused on the goals they feel passionately about achieving.

Adults learn differently than children, and trainers need to understand adult learning theory to help trainees to build skills and realize their potential growth.

Training

Specialized, workplace-specific training for current employees is an ongoing process. Furthermore, there are several types of training, each addressing a different need.

Some training focuses on existing conditions and circumstances; other types focus on changing current employees' behaviors in performing their current jobs. Still other training deals more specifically with accommodating changes in the work environment. For example, when new machines are introduced, new software is added to computer networks, new production methods become available, and/or new organizational procedures and systems are implemented, employees must be trained in the proper use of those procedures and systems.[1]

Before any training is done, however, prepare a comprehensive needs assessment. First, identify what skills are needed. Next, assess your current staff against the level of those skills. There are many ways to create a training needs assessment. Certainly the manager, from his or her vantage point, can evaluate the employee's strengths and areas for development based on actual work product and personal observations.

Leah Moran Rampy, PhD, reminds us that, although managers' views of employees' development needs are important, they're not comprehensive. Peers, direct reports, and customers can provide important feedback about a person's skill, behavior, and attitude. A 360-degree feedback process—involving those who work "above," "below," and "with" the employee—can enrich the assessment and show how others perceive him or her.

Managers can obtain 360-degree feedback using published, standardized assessment tools; customized, organization-specific processes; or interviews by the manager, an HR professional, or an external coach/consultant. A cautionary note: If those providing feedback assume that the information will be used "against" the employee in any way, such as in a performance review, they often temper their answers. Most people don't want to cause trouble for the employee (and some may want to, subjectively).

Therefore, 360-degree feedback is most useful when respondents are offered anonymity and an HR professional or trained coach helps the employee interpret the feedback. Changing employee behavior or encouraging training is more likely when this feedback is part of an overall development process that includes support from senior management to complete and sustain it. Used responsibly and thoughtfully, 360-degree feedback can provide insights to employees about how they are perceived, and help target key opportunities for development.

A 360-degree approach, customer feedback, and a self-review can provide a fuller assessment of performance and/or training needs.

Sample Needs Assessment

For each of the following areas of skill, knowledge, and ability, please make two judgments. First, rate the importance of each item to your current job requirements by choosing a number from 1 to 4 (4 = very important; 3 = important; 2 = somewhat important; 1 = not important or not relevant). Second, indicate your current level of proficiency in each area, again choosing a number from 1 to 4 (4 = very proficient; 3 = proficient; 2 = somewhat proficient; 1 = not proficient).

	Importance	**Proficiency**

Technical skills:
Computer literacy

Marketing

Writing/editing

Strategic planning

Finance/accounting

Analytical/problem-solving skills:
Decision-making

Troubleshooting

Research and evaluation

Oral communications skills:

Meeting facilitation

Speaking/presenting

    What other issues do you need to work on to be more effective in your role?

    Reproduced with permission from Ann Casso, an organizational development specialist.

Tailor your plan

    After reviewing information about the employee's needs, develop an action plan involving instructional design (learning objectives, content, and interactive exercises) followed by implementation and evaluation. Managers can purchase off-the-shelf training programs, create the course from scratch in-house, or identify a trainer who will customize sessions according to the individuals and their needs.

    One size does not fit all. Consider whether on-the-job training, apprenticeship training, informal learning, audiovisual tools, lectures, workshops, simulated training, long-distance courses, computer-based training, or a combination of several methods will work best.

    Different learning styles also matter. Each individual learns best when trained in his or her optimal style, and the way in which information is presented influences how well a person receives, accepts, and adapts the information. Coaching and counseling should present the information in an optimal way for each person's learning style, and it is the manager's responsibility to construct and deliver the training accordingly.

There are dozens of learning styles, but the following list encompasses some of those most applicable to the workplace.

✓ Some people are visual learners (they rely on visualizing, or creating mental images), whereas others are auditory (they rely on listening to presented information).

✓ Some prefer to talk rather than to think; others need to think and process information first, then talk about it.

✓ Some prefer to work intently on a task with no interruptions or noise; others have shorter attention spans and welcome interruptions or breaks.

✓ Some prefer to ask questions or read directions first, then plunge in, whereas others prefer to jump first, then ask questions or read directions.

✓ Some prefer "the big picture," or global perspective; others like a step-by-step, linear view.

✓ Some people solve problems quickly; others deliberate more.

Remember. Ongoing development has been recognized as an important aspect of employee retention, and it should *not* be underestimated. To quote a Chinese proverb: If you want one year of prosperity, grow grain. If you want 10 years of prosperity, grow trees. If you want 100 years of prosperity, grow people.

Mentoring

Joanne Lozar Glenn, the author of *Mentor Me*, tells us that, as a manager, you have another valuable tool for retaining employees: formal or informal mentoring. The demand for mentoring is growing, especially among younger employees. Research suggests that those in the so-called millennial generation (born 1977–1998) have high expectations for themselves and their careers, and they learn best from the "coaching" style.[2]

Your employees want mentoring in two areas:

1. **The skills they need to succeed on the job.** Ongoing training and development should include your one-on-one coaching, based on your own experience.

2. **The skills they need to build a satisfying career.** Here, you serve as both a role model and a networker for your employees. Share your own struggles and successes. Invite employees to attend important meetings with you, and then to attend future meetings in your place. Expose them to other successful professionals inside and outside your organization, and encourage them to discuss their own career development.

You can also inspire employees to mentor themselves by encouraging them to be their own best advocates in the workplace. Here's how:

✓ Teach employees to recognize and play to their strengths.

✓ Help them address their own mistakes with a sense of humor, or at least with grace.

✓ Challenge employees to increase creative control of their jobs, and take a proactive approach to performance reviews.

✓ Help them build a portfolio that showcases their best work, and teach them the subtle arts of self-promotion.

✓ Introduce them to a mentor other than yourself who can help them work through issues in a short-term, highly focused encounter, such as handling career plateaus or transitions, or navigating office politics.

Evaluation

Assessing training effectiveness often entails using the four-level model developed by Donald Kirkpatrick (1994).[3] According to this model, evaluation should always begin with level one, and then, as time and budget allow, should move sequentially through levels two, three, and four. Information from each prior level serves as a base for the next level's evaluation. Thus, each successive level requires a more rigorous, time-consuming analysis, but each also represents a more precise measure of the training's effectiveness.

Level 1 evaluation—reactions

Just as the word implies, evaluation at this level measures how participants in a training program react to it. It attempts to answer questions regarding the participants' perceptions: Did they like it? Was the material relevant to their work? This type of evaluation is often called a "smile sheet." According to Kirkpatrick, every program should at least be evaluated at this level to provide for the improvement of a training program. In addition, the participants' reactions have important consequences for learning level two. Although a positive reaction does not guarantee learning, a negative reaction almost certainly reduces its possibility.

Sample Participant Evaluation

For the following questions, please answer: strongly agree, agree, not sure, disagree, or strongly disagree.

The length of this session was appropriate.

The session was relevant to my work and me.

The trainer was knowledgeable about the content.

The session's pace was appropriate.

The session was well organized.

I would recommend this session to others.

What was the most important thing you learned today?

How will you use the information you gained during this session while on the job?

What other training or professional development would help you be more effective in your job?

Please provide additional comments about the session and the trainer.

Level 2 evaluation—learning

Assessing at this level moves the evaluation beyond learner satisfaction and attempts to assess the extent to which students have advanced in skills, knowledge, or attitude. Measurement at this level is more difficult and laborious than at level one. Methods range from formal to informal testing to team assessment and self-assessment. If possible, participants take the test or the assessment before the training (pre-test) and after training (post-test) to determine the amount of learning that has occurred.

University of Maryland Libraries Questionnaire

The University of Maryland Libraries has designed a very effective form that is sent out months after training. Among its questions:

What knowledge or skills did you learn at this workshop?

Have you used or applied the knowledge or skills from the workshop?

If yes, how have you used the skills? If no, why not?

Are there other skills you wish had been taught at this workshop? If yes, what skills?

This workshop has made a positive impact on how I do my job (choose strongly agree, agree, neutral, disagree, or strongly disagree).

This workshop would be beneficial to others who do similar types of work (same choices as previous question).

Level 3 evaluation—transfer

This level measures the transfer that has occurred in learners' behavior due to the training program. Evaluating at this level attempts to answer the question, "Are the newly acquired skills, knowledge, or attitude being used in the everyday environment of the learner?" For many trainers, this level represents the truest assessment of a program's effectiveness. However, measuring at this level is difficult, as it is often impossible to predict when the change in behavior will occur, and thus requires important decisions in terms of when to evaluate, how often to evaluate, and how to evaluate.

Level 4 evaluation—results

Frequently thought of as the bottom line, this level measures the success of the program in terms that managers and executives can understand: increased production, improved quality, decreased costs, reduced frequency of accidents, increased sales, and even higher profits or return on investment. From a business and organizational perspective, this is the overall reason for a training program, yet results at this level are not typically addressed. Determining results in financial terms is difficult to measure, and they are hard to link directly with training.

Main message for managers

It's important for experienced employees to improve the skills and knowledge that help them function more effectively and grow. It is also important to effect change in your workplace in order to continue to grow and remain competitive.

Peter Senge, author of *The Fifth Discipline: The Art and Practice of The Learning Organization,* defines these as "organizations where people continually expand their capacity to create the results they truly desire, where new and expansive patterns of thinking are nurtured, where collective aspiration is set free, and where people are continually learning to see the whole together."[4]

Anne Hull of Hull Strategies, LLC, reminds us that, to be successful, managers must *develop* employees—at least in part because it frees the managers to function less as problem-solvers and more as managers and leaders. Before training begins, discuss with the employee what each of you wants to learn from the training. Align the training objectives with both your department's goals and the employee's career goals. Identify specific ways in which you expect the employee to use his or her newly acquired skills on the job.

However, beware of training that neither changes behavior nor improves performance. It *is* possible to make permanent, measurable improvements in individual performance that has a positive impact on business results. But, says organizational development specialist and trainer Jane Pettit of GroupWorks, this almost never happens, because most managers:

✓ Neglect to follow up assessment and training programs with adequate reinforcement. They don't understand that it takes months of on-the-job application and reinforcement for trainees to absorb and consistently apply a new skill.

✓ Present training programs as events. Performance improvement has to be an ongoing process to reinforce what is learned.

✓ Fail to hold themselves responsible for the coaching role. Because most performance improvement occurs in the workplace, the employee's direct supervisor needs to be involved: communicating expectations, observing, encouraging, supporting, giving feedback, coaching, and holding the employee accountable.

Finally, take a proactive, personal approach to your employees' development: Find ways to mentor them. As in all good business relationships, mentoring is a two-way street. Be open to not only what employees need to learn, but also to what they can teach you in return.

Chapter 5
Useful Performance Evaluations

Lack of feedback is the number one reason for performance problems.
—Leigh F. Branham, author, *The 7 Hidden Reasons Employees Leave: How to Recognize the Subtle Signs and Act Before It's Too Late*

Performance appraisals have been around for more than 100 years, but we're still not getting them right! Too often, the employee listens as the manager dominates the conversation. An effective performance review works similar to a walkie-talkie.

What is a performance appraisal?

Most employees want to know how they are performing. They care about whether they're making progress—both in the company and, especially for younger staff, in their careers. They want to do their work the right way.

Employees have the right to know what their managers expect from them, and they're entitled to learn how to meet those expectations. That's why managers must have frequent, ongoing communication with employees to evaluate their performance. The performance appraisal is merely the culmination of all those short and long discussions throughout the year.

Whatever system an organization uses—formal or not— appraisal meetings should reflect the organization's culture, just as dress does. Consider the difference between the culture of a bank, where business attire is required, and that of a graphic-design studio, where baseball caps and jeans are the norm.

A performance appraisal is:

✓ One of a manager's most important responsibilities.

✓ An ongoing process, not a single event.

✓ The culmination of brief meetings between manager and employee during the entire performance period.

✓ An objective way to determine whether the employee has met predetermined expectations and how well he or she has done.

✓ A tool to clarify current expectations and set new ones, and to explore new responsibilities for the employee.

Benefits of a performance appraisal

For the organization

✓ Communicates corporate goals.

✓ Provides management with information for making decisions about staff.

✓ Provides objective basis for raises, promotions, training, and other personnel actions.

✓ Strengthens working relationships.

✓ Improves overall productivity.

✓ Provides documentation for inquiries, claims, or actions.

For the manager

✓ Builds management skills.

✓ Develops and improves rapport with employees.

✓ Identifies and rewards the best performers.

✓ Identifies employees who need coaching or training.

✓ Improves individual employee productivity.

✓ Helps identify general training needs.

✓ Demonstrates fairness to employees.

✓ Improves group morale.

For the employee

✓ Conveys how well he or she is performing.

✓ Provides recognition for accomplishments.

✓ Allows for two-way communication on goals and performance.

✓ Encourages taking responsibility for performance and progress.

✓ Helps set goals and focus efforts.

✓ Provides opportunities for career development and improvement.

Five hallmarks of effective performance appraisals

✓ *Active employee participation.* Encourage the employee to describe issues and his or her feelings and concerns during the review period.

✓ *Positive attitude.* Establish an upbeat tone that will make the employee want to participate; if dicey performance issues are discussed, be helpful and constructive in suggesting how to improve.

✓ *Mutual problem-solving.* You and the employee work together to find solutions.

✓ *Mutual goal-setting.* Collaborate with the employee to set objectives for him or her to achieve in the next review period; aim for goals with measurable results.

✓ *Clear examples.* Demonstrate or describe the behaviors and results that illustrate your ratings and assessments.

Types of appraisals

✓ *Checklist appraisal:* The supervisor chooses from a list of behavioral descriptions. Sometimes items are weighted to reflect importance.

✓ *Critical-incident appraisal:* Focusing on key behaviors that define aspects of the job, the supervisor provides specific, work-related anecdotes conveying what an employee did or didn't do.

✓ *Essay appraisal:* In a written narrative, the supervisor describes an employee's strengths, areas for improvement, achievement of goals, plans for professional development, and so forth.

✓ *Forced-choice appraisal:* From two or more specific statements, the supervisor selects the one that best describes the employee. In a variation of this form, the appraiser selects a statement that is "most like" the employee and another that is "least like" the employee.

✓ *Graphic-scale appraisal:* Also known as the Adjective Rating Scale, this is one of the oldest and most popular methods of evaluating performance. This type of appraisal is used to assess dimension/performance factors. On a scale, the appraiser marks points that best describe the employee. For example, under Initiative, you mark how the employee does not meet expectations, partially meets expectations, meets expectations, exceeds expectations, or far exceeds expectations. Generally, there is a "comments" section where the appraiser gives specific details to support the rating.

✓ *Group order ranking:* The supervisor ranks each employee who reports to him or her so as to place the employee within a group, such as the top third of performers.

✓ *Individual ranking:* The supervisor ranks all employees according to their work performance, from highest to lowest. There can be no ties.

✓ *Paired comparison:* The supervisor compares each employee with every other member of the group, ranking employees' performances by counting the number of times any individual is the first ranked among all.

Do's and don'ts of performance appraisals

"Great managers excel at 'holding up the mirror.' They excel at giving performance feedback.... Whatever their style, whatever their tools of choice, they are all trying to do the same thing: to hold up the mirror so that the employee has a chance to discover a little more about who he is, how he works, and the footprint he leaves on the world."

—Marcus Buckingham and Curt Coffman, authors of *First Break All the Rules*

Do…

✓ Reassure your employees by building on strengths. Give them confidence.

✓ Be specific about both strengths and weaknesses in discussing performance.

✓ Draw employees out by asking thought-provoking, open-ended questions. Then LISTEN—with warmth and genuine interest. Restate or rephrase the employees' statements to make sure you understand.

✓ Keep the focus of the discussion on track.

✓ Talk about job results.

✓ Close the review properly: Summarize, plan for improvement and changes, and write down the plans and agreements between you and the employee.

Don't...

✓ Use negative words or too many negative criticisms.

✓ Convey a "you vs. me" or a condescending attitude.

✓ Give insincere or excessive praise.

✓ Use generalities that cannot be backed up by specific examples.

✓ Dominate the conversation; employees should talk for about 60 percent of the meeting time.

✓ Appear hurried. Be sure to plan the time and avoid interruptions.

Smarter goals

You can improve on the pro forma goals that often dominate performance reviewees. Remember: Smarter goal-setting produces better goal achieving!

S = Specific
M = Measurable
A = Attainable
R = Relevant
T = Time-based
E = Engaging
R = Reinforcing

The five components of a performance appraisal meeting

1. Planning and preparation

Before the meeting, make sure you're familiar with the evaluation form and the rating structure. Whether your company uses grades, a sliding scale, or some other kind of quantitative measure, you may need to explain how it works as well as the criteria for each rating step.

Reread the job description for the employee's position: Is it still accurate, or have the employee's responsibilities changed?

Review individual goals set during the previous evaluation to assess how well the employee met or is meeting them. Does he or she understand your expectations? What are the employee's strengths and weaknesses? Does he or she contribute to the group's mission?

To make the review objective, collect examples of the employee's work that illustrate each point you make. For example, show him or her the report with too many errors in basic grammar.

Now you're ready to start filling out the evaluation form. Draft it in private, put it aside for a day, and review it for clarity and tone from the employee's point of view. Be prepared to justify the rating with specific examples of either work product or incidents that reflect the employee's results or behavior.

Plan the details of the discussion: What work, behavior, or problem-solving will you compliment? What will you point out as needing improvement, and why?

Remember, though, that you're not preparing for a solo performance! Managers need to think about how to involve employees in the entire evaluation process, including the formal performance appraisal. Ideally, the employee should do most of the talking and, similar to the manager, should evaluate his or her performance before the meeting.

This is the time for the employee to focus on the future: What do I want? What do I need to achieve it? How does this job contribute to developing my career? The appraisal meeting is an investment in his or her professional development.

When you schedule the meeting, choose a day and time when neither of you is under pressure. Allow enough time for a two-way discussion, and encourage the employee to write a self-evaluation; even though it's usually optional, you should explain, in positive terms, why both evaluations are valuable. They're designed to help employees gauge their own performance and to learn how they're doing from their supervisors' point of view.

Set a deadline to make sure you have a chance to read the self-evaluation before the meeting. (If it differs from yours on important points, be prepared to discuss the two versions, including which is more accurate and why.) Finally, arrange to hold the meeting in a private space—preferably on "neutral turf" outside your office or away from the building.

Before the meeting, carefully read the review again, checking for fairness and objectivity; make sure you have based the evaluation strictly on the employee's performance. Verify that the document contains the ABCs: It should be Accurate, Behavioral, Complete, and Consistent.

Check that you have the examples you'll need for the discussion close by.

2. Starting the meeting

Set a warm tone—informal but professional—from the beginning, so that the employee feels at ease and comfortable. However, avoid small talk, and move right into reassurance if the employee seems anxious. If you are planning to bring up many positive points, do so! That's an instant stress-reducer. But don't say it unless it's true.

Another approach is to emphasize that it's a routine meeting, one that every employee and supervisor in the organization has every year. Or you can share your own experience with evaluations: Were you wary the first time? Did your supervisor say or do something that lowered the tension?

At this point, elaborate on the value of the meeting; it's an investment in the employee's professional development. Not only is it a time to resolve any problems, but it also ensures that you're on the same track in setting realistic, workable goals and priorities; your feedback is intended to help the employee succeed.

Briefly outline what ground you want to cover in the meeting, in what order, how the meeting will be structured, and what you want to accomplish. This not only lets the employee know what to expect, but it also provides an opening for him or her to raise issues you haven't mentioned.

If you haven't already given the employee your written appraisal and allowed him or her enough time to read it, do so now. (And if you haven't already received the self-evaluation, you can both read simultaneously.)

Encourage the employee to share his or her impression of what you wrote, which should lead into discussing any major differences between your evaluations.

3. The discussion

Now that we've covered the structure and overall aim of the appraisal meeting, you might think, "Fine, but what do I *say?*"

First, ask open-ended questions to get a general reaction. Many reviewers start with, "How do you think things have been going?" or, "What would you do differently?"

Let the employee talk; listen, and try not to interrupt. Nature gave us two ears and one mouth so that we would use them proportionately. You want to empower the employee, not assert your superiority.

Describe the employee's job in terms of the big picture. What is its purpose, and how does it affect, and reflect, the organization's success? Some aspects of the job are bound to be less fulfilling than others; why are they important?

Review the employee's significant accomplishments; nothing beats praise and credit for building confidence, driving discussion, and reinforcing good performance ratings. You might begin with a statement such as:

✓ "You've made important contributions this year."
✓ "I was very impressed by the way you handled _____."
✓ "You've been more conscientious about _____."
✓ "I was pleased to see _____."

Then you can move on to the form. Work your way through each section of it, using it as a tool to encourage discussion. Remember to focus on the employee's job performance, not personal characteristics.

Consider asking questions such as:

✓ "What have I done to help—or hinder—your job performance?"
✓ "What can I do in the next review period to help you achieve/improve?"
✓ "What conditions here enable you—or make it hard—to do your best work?" "How would you like to receive suggestions for improving your work?"
✓ "What do you want most from your job?"
✓ "How can I help you reach your career goals?"

When you discuss areas where the employee's performance falls short, use phrases such as "I was concerned _____." Be prepared to back up your points with specific examples, including the tangible ones you collected when you wrote the evaluation. Stay calm, and don't express your constructive criticism in such a way that you seriously disturb a good employee, remember that, in the end, you're trying to encourage improvement.

Ask the employee for suggestions on how to improve his or her performance, and describe specific actions he or she can take to do so.

The aim at this point is mutual understanding, not necessarily complete agreement. You can agree to disagree, and you should explain that is why there is a section for employees' comments.

At a National Health Service Hospital in the United Kingdom, where supervisors and employees jointly set work objectives, employees reported finding the process beneficial so long as they were actively engaged in the process. They reported that the objectives they set for themselves were more interesting and challenging than those set by their supervisors.[1]

4. Closing

It's just as important to end the meeting in a professional and positive manner as it was to start that way. You want the employee to leave the discussion with a positive impression of the process.

Ask him or her to summarize the discussion you just had; make sure you are on the same page regarding the important points.

If the employee introduced points you hadn't considered while writing the appraisal, apologize for your oversight and say you'd like a few days to consider how this information might affect your evaluation. Then go and do it.

With the employee, agree on a plan for the future. Write goals for the next evaluation cycle that are specific, measurable, challenging but achievable, and time-specific. You can offer to help him or her reach those goals.

Think about training, skills development, new opportunities, or added responsibilities for the employee. Engage the employee in the plan for his or her future.

Share your ideas on where the department is headed. Make sure the employee knows how important he or she will be to helping the department reach its new goals.

As you close, ask the employee for any last thoughts or reactions. Consider asking:

✓ "What have you learned?"

✓ "Were you surprised?"

✓ "Was the appraisal fair?"

Remind the employee that, if he or she has any additional reactions later, your door is always open. Close the meeting on a friendly note, and remind the employee that he or she is an important part of the team, whose performance affects your department and the organization. Encourage him or her, and be sure to express appreciation for good work and for participating in the evaluation process.

If the meeting wasn't positive, allow the employee to disagree with any points you made. Check the procedures in your organization for formally responding to the appraisal, and present as many options to the employee as you can, such as having him or her document the areas of disagreement concerning the performance appraisal form, or on a separate sheet to be attached; or discuss the issue(s) with your own supervisor or with Human Resources.

Don't forget the final administrative step: Have the employee sign and date the form, explaining that it indicates only that the two of you have discussed the appraisal. Stress confidentiality, and tell him or her where the form will be kept.

Remind the employee that you'll continue to give feedback throughout the year and welcome any questions about his or her performance as well.

5. Follow-up

It's crucial that managers follow up on any commitments they've made to employees. If you told the employee you'd provide special support or find a training course for him or her, make sure you do it!

Don't forget to deliver the signed forms confidentially to wherever your organization keeps them.

A helpful next step is to assess your own approach in the appraisal meeting. Make notes about what worked and what didn't, and keep them where you'll find them for review before your next meeting.

Immediately start observing behavior, collecting work samples, and making notes for the next performance appraisal meeting. What system or procedure you use doesn't matter; what does is that you set up a process for tracking performance. This way you'll never be caught without specific examples to support your ratings—a hallmark of effective appraisals.

Ratings errors

Ratings errors arise from techniques that mislead or blind supervisors as they undertake performance appraisals. Everyone who conducts appraisals must guard against these pitfalls, which distort objective reality—favorably or unfavorably.

Here are nine of the more common ratings errors:

✓ Centralizing—Clustering everyone in the middle performance-rating categories. It's an easy way to avoid extreme rankings, either good or bad, but it's wrong.

✓ Favoritism—Overlooking the flaws or exaggerating the achievements of favored employees, especially popular ones.

✓ Grouping—Excusing substandard performance or behavior because it is widespread. ("Everyone does it.")

✓ The halo/horns effect—Letting one characteristic or work product—positive or negative—affect your overall assessment.

✓ Guilt by association—Rating someone based on the company he or she keeps rather than on his or her work. Watch out for the "halo" version of this error as well (letting your appraisal of one person's performance dictate your appraisal of another's).

✓ Holding a grudge—Be conscious of your personal feelings about an employee and put them firmly aside. Never make an employee pay for past behavior—it might land you in court.

✓ Bias—Whether legally prohibited (race, national origin, sex, religion, age, veteran status, disability) or not (hair color, weight, height, intelligence, grooming), bias is prejudice and has no place in assessing job performance. Guard against letting your personal attitudes intrude on the process.

✓ Shortening time—The specific work you are rating should be representative of the entire review period; don't focus on only recent performance.

✓ The sunflower effect—Rating everyone high, regardless of performance, to make you look good or give more compensation.

Keep it legal

Managing and evaluating employees improperly can quickly move a manager into the legal arena. Potential legal pitfalls surround every discussion about performance. Among their causes:

✓ Unclear communication.

✓ Lack of concrete, specific goals.

✓ Improper or incomplete record-keeping.

✓ Inaccurate performance ratings.

✓ Failure to follow up on commitments.

Remember that what you write on a performance appraisal form could be tested in court. Protect your organization and yourself by making sure that you clearly communicate expectations of job performance and maintain accurate written records. Always base your evaluation on specific, job-related behaviors only. (See Chapter 9.)

Reviewing the reviewer

Remember that every performance appraisal that fails to motivate is a lost opportunity for both the manager and the employee. A poorly handled one will decrease productivity, lower morale, and be counterproductive.

It doesn't have to be that way! Many organizations' performance appraisals are constructive and strengthen workplace culture because they remind employees of their value to the employer. The performance appraisal is the best management tool you have to improve the employee's performance.

Main message for managers

Performance appraisals aren't always easy or fun, but every performance discussion that fails to motivate (or worse) is a lost opportunity for both the manager and the employee. A poorly handled review will decrease productivity and lower morale; it can even be counterproductive to building good relationships with your employees.

If conducted properly, performance appraisals can be constructive, strengthen the company, and add value to you and your employees.

And the way to do them properly is to keep communicating with your direct reports all year, all the time. It was discovered a long time ago that feedback is critical in order to maintain good performance. Managers have to develop the good habit of providing continuous feedback to employees.

That way, when the formal annual or semi-annual performance appraisal comes up, there are no surprises; the discussion is merely the summary of all the conversations (short and long) you've had with the employee during the entire performance cycle. Your responsibility is to involve the employee in the entire appraisal process, including the discussion that concludes it.

Change is no easy task, but the tools provided in this chapter will sharpen your management and evaluation skills. To do it, you'll have to be willing to challenge yourself and address:

✓ Your willingness to give up comfortable, familiar, but ineffective ways of thinking and behaving about performance management.

✓ Your willingness to make the time to read about and practice new techniques for performance management.

Remember: Continuous feedback is an effective management tool, so start talking!

Chapter 6
Benefits

By Michael Strand

Write your injuries in dust, your benefits in marble.

—Benjamin Franklin, American statesman, scientist, philosopher, author, and inventor

Government-mandated benefits

Based on an evolving national commitment to provide workers with basic welfare and security, both federal and state laws require several benefits. Individual states and other jurisdictions may require benefits, such as minimum wage and continued insurance after layoff or firing, that are more generous than the federal requirements. Have your legal counsel check all relevant employment laws.

Social Security and Medicare

Social Security replaces a portion of income upon retirement, based on a formula of earnings and years worked (eligibility starts at age 62). Medicare, a health insurance benefit, provides basic protection against the cost of healthcare (eligibility at age 65). Employers and employees pay equal portions of the Social Security and Medicare taxes.

If an employee has multiple employers, it may be important to track total earnings each year because the Social Security tax is subject to a dollar limit (adjusted annually for inflation). The employer's responsibility for withholding and matching the Social Security tax ends once that limit is reached. There is no current earnings limit for the Medicare portion of the tax.

Unemployment insurance

Unemployment insurance provides compensation to qualified workers during periods of involuntary unemployment. Each state administers the premiums, claims, and payment of unemployment benefits through either a state agency or a qualified insurance company. Nevertheless, unemployment insurance laws are heavily guided by federal standards. The Federal Unemployment Tax Act (FUTA) imposes an annual tax on the first $7,000 of wages paid to each employee. The state tax depends on state guidelines, which may include the employer's unemployment-claims history.

To minimize unemployment claims, employers should: have in hand a written statement specifying the reason each employee is resigning his or her position (employees who are laid off will probably be eligible; eligibility for those who are fired depends on the circumstances); ensure there is sufficient cause to fire or lay off an employee; respond promptly and thoroughly to inquiries from the state unemployment agency; challenge an agency's decision to grant unemployment benefits if you believe they are not deserved; and, if necessary, present evidence at an unemployment hearing.

Workers' compensation

Workers' compensation is paid to employees injured on the job for loss of compensation and for medical payments to a provider for treating the injury. States may differ on the minimum number of employees necessary to require employers' participation in the workers compensation program. States generally administer workers compensation through either a state agency or a qualified insurance company.

A primary purpose of workers' compensation is to relieve the employer from liability for worker injuries, so long as the employer was not negligent.

Family and medical leave

The federal Family and Medical Leave Act (FMLA) requires employers with 50 or more employees to allow eligible employees up to 12 weeks of unpaid leave during a 12-month period for treatment of a serious health condition of the employee or the employee's immediate family, the birth of a child, or acquiring a child through adoption or foster care. The employee must meet certain conditions to be eligible, as well as other requirements. (As with unemployment insurance, some states have more generous FMLA leave provisions.)

State disability income insurance

Some states require employers to provide temporary disability insurance for employees. (See disability insurance on page 87.)

Core benefits

Nearly all employers, large and small, offer some basic benefitsthat provide paid time off. Somewhat less prevalent, but no less important, are health insurance, life insurance, disability insurance, and retirement plans.

Paid time off

As a societal tradition, most employers offer holidays, vacation, sick leave, and other days off to be competitive with other employers and foster a mentally healthy workforce. Organizations' paid-time-off plans are usually administered internally. Even if payroll management is not computerized, a file of basic time and attendance cards should be sufficient to adequately administer eligibility for and use of paid time off.

Holidays

Although no federal or state laws require employers to offer paid or unpaid holidays, almost all organizations do. Their selection of holidays can vary depending on the industry (construction, retail sales, trade association, civil service, and so on). The most widely observed paid holidays are New Year's Day, Memorial Day, Independence Day, Labor Day, Thanksgiving Day, and Christmas Day. Other holidays often added to the list include Martin Luther King Jr. Day, President's Day, Columbus Day, Election Day, Veterans Day, the Friday after Thanksgiving, and Christmas Eve.

Although the observance of some holidays is designed to create three-day weekends, others occasionally fall on and are celebrated during a weekend. To address these circumstances, many employers' written policies state, "Unless otherwise notified, a holiday that falls on a Saturday will be observed on the previous Friday; a holiday that falls on a Sunday will be observed on the following Monday."

Whether to extend holiday pay to part-time employees often depends on how critical the part-timers are to the organization and the number of hours they usually work. When extending paid time off—including holidays—to part-timers, employers often prorate the time paid. For example, six hours of holiday pay for part-timers who regularly work at least 30 hours a week; four hours for those who regularly work at least 20 hours; and two hours for part-timers who regularly work at least 10 hours.

Vacation

Vacation days are usually accumulated through accrual throughout a unit of time, such as pay period, month, or year. Employers usually require advance notice and supervisor approval of vacation time. They do not typically approve more vacation time than the employee has already accrued.

Annual vacation accrual amounts to between one and four or more weeks a year, depending on how long the employee has worked for the organization, the rank of his or her position, and (less often) other factors. A new employee may accrue one or two weeks of vacation time in the first year, though most employees have to wait three to five years or more before they accrue additional weeks.

Some organizations limit the amount of vacation time employees are allowed to "carry" in order to encourage them to take their time off, which is intended for rest and relaxation away from the workplace. The limits vary from the somewhat draconian "use-or-lose" policy (usually by year) to several years. Nearly all organizations pay employees for their accrued but unused vacation time when he or she leaves the employer. Because of this, organizational accounting must enter accrued vacation as a liability from one year to the next.

As with holidays, firms that rely heavily on their part-time employees may allow prorated vacation accrual. It is unusual, however, for organizations to prorate vacation accrual to those who work less than 20 hours a week.

Sick leave

Traditionally, sick leave is paid time off for an employee's own illness. With the advent of "family-friendly" employee-benefit plans, more organizations are extending the use of sick leave to allow employees paid time off to care for other members of the immediate family when they have a temporary illness.

Typically, sick leaves accrues periodically for a total of six to 12 days a year. Organizations that provide disability insurance often impose a limit on sick leave accrual—but, unlike vacation time, unused sick leave is not typically paid to employees who leave. Thus, there are no balance-sheet ramifications to carrying over sick leave from one period to the next. Some organizations have a sick leave buy-back program, in which employees may convert a portion of their unused sick leave to vacation or cash.

Having a written policy on the use of sick leave helps minimize the possibility of abuse. The policy should have guidelines for when and whom an employee should notify in case of illness, and it may require supportive documentation, such as a doctor's note, if the absence is for more than a specified number of days. The policy should also describe the disciplinary consequences in case of a persistent problem with sick-leave absences. And some organizations have a policy of not paying sick leave once an employee has given notice of resignation.

A major problem with sick leave is that it is often unscheduled, placing a burden on other employees. Some employers are combining vacation and sick leave accrual in a paid-leave "bank." This can reduce the organization's costs for administrative time and absenteeism.

Here's an example of how an organization can convert from a vacation and sick-leave plan to a paid-time-off plan. Say the former plan provided 10 days of vacation and 10 days of sick leave per year. Under the new paid-time-off plan, half the former annual accrual of sick leave is added to the vacation leave.

Thus, each employee receives 15 days of paid time off per year. Employees who don't use their sick leave will love this change. Employees who routinely use all or most of their sick leave will hate this change. Whom do you want to please?

It may be prudent to allow employees who have accumulated significant sick leave hours to use those hours within a limited period (say, two to three years). To retain some control over that use, the organization may require employees who want to use the old, accumulated sick leave hours to first use two days of paid-time-off hours.

Personal leave

Personal leave is time off for personal reasons that are typically not included in sick leave or vacation leave. Personal leave usually amounts to one to three days a year, typically provided on a "use-it-or-lose-it" basis. It's often used for religious observances; that way, employees who feel "forced" to take off Christmas Day don't demand to substitute a different religious holiday (or days).

Bereavement leave

Bereavement (or funeral) leave is paid leave for an employee to attend the funeral of a family member and/or attend to estate-related activities of a deceased family member. The length of bereavement leave is usually up to three work days, depending on travel time and estate circumstances. Some organizations' policies limit the type of family members for whom employees can take bereavement leave, such as "immediate family" or "children, spouses, and parents." If the relationship to the deceased relative falls outside those limits, employees can usually take paid personal days or vacation time.

Health insurance

Health insurance (including hospitalization and medical benefits) is probably the most contentious of the core benefits because of the dramatic increase in premium costs. As those increases mount, more small businesses are dropping coverage or, at the least, employees are paying a greater portion of the premium—especially for family and dependent coverage.

There are three basic types of health insurance plans:

1. **Indemnity or traditional plans:** Employees can see any physician, physicians receive a fee for service, there are limits on the dollar amount of coverage over time, annual deductibles are common, and the premium is usually more expensive than other types of healthcare plans.

2. **HMO:** Health Maintenance Organizations restrict the employee's choice of physicians to those specifically in the HMO group, physicians receive a fixed fee per patient or a salary, and cost control mechanisms are prevalent (for example, the use of nurse practitioners to screen patients, or wellness and preventive programs).

3. **PPO:** Preferred Provider Organizations are a blend of traditional and HMO plans. They have contractual arrangements with physicians, who agree to fee schedules and other plan requirements, and employees can choose from among more physicians than under an HMO plan, but fewer than under an indemnity plan. Employees may, however, be able to see physicians outside the PPO plan network after deductibles and/or with copayments.

Consumer-driven healthcare plans are a relatively recent type of health coverage that attempt to address the issue of rising premiums. These plans, known as FSAs (flexible spending accounts), HRAs (health reimbursement accounts), or HSAs (health savings accounts) have two common characteristics: (1) premiums under a high-deductible health plan are a fraction of those under a conventional health plan. The high-deductible plan does not begin to cover healthcare costs until the annual deductible (for example, $2,000 individual/$4,000 family) is reached; (2) concurrently, the employer makes contributions to the designated employee reimbursement, spending, or savings account. Funds in this account meet healthcare costs after the deductible is reached each year.

In theory, the initial cost to the employer of the high-deductible premium, plus the contributions to the FSA, HRA, or HSA, is no greater than that of conventional health insurance; employees are not likely to reach the annual deductible; the funds building up in the account are enough to meet expenses; and the account builds significantly from year to year, to the point where few additional contributions are needed to cover the insured adequately.

COBRA

The Consolidated Omnibus Budget Reconciliation Act (CO-BRA) requires employers with 20 or more employees to provide continued healthcare coverage to individuals and qualified beneficiaries after termination of employment, for up to 18 or 36 months, depending on the circumstances. Employers are required to notify employees who are leaving, and their family members, of their CO-BRA right to continued coverage. However, at least 100 percent of the premium must be paid by the former employee. Some states have more generous COBRA provisions.

Life insurance

Employer-provided group life insurance has become a common feature of the employee-benefit package. Most employers provide some level of life insurance. Often, life insurance is "bundled" with another benefit, such as health insurance. Traditionally, group life insurance was considered "burial insurance," so the expected amount was minimal. More recently, expectations have risen significantly, so that the minimal level of coverage is $10,000, with more firms offering one year's pay up to $50,000. Employers can provide up to $50,000 of group life insurance coverage to employees on a nontaxable basis. The value of coverage above $50,000 is considered a taxable benefit to the employee. The IRS set the $50,000 ceiling years ago so that the plan would not discriminate in favor of the more highly paid employees. Since then, salaries have risen significantly, and employers have begun to provide life insurance worth more than $50,000.

There are two very basic types of life insurance:

1. **Permanent life** (also known as variable life, whole life, universal life, or yet-to-be named variations) builds a redemption value into the insurance plan. Because permanent life insurance is expensive, few employers provide it.

2. **Term insurance** is in force for a specific time period, such as five years, 15 years, and so forth. Employers typically purchase term insurance that covers employees during their employment only, with such policies as, "Life insurance coverage begins the first of the month after date of hire and ends the first of the month after termination of employment."

For an employee group whose age span is representative of the working population, the premium for group term insurance is considerably less than life insurance that the employees could purchase individually—that is, group term life insurance can be a valuable addition to the core benefits package. And few employees will opt for coverage above $50,000, because they must pay income tax and Social Security tax on the "excess" coverage.

To calculate the amount of excess insurance coverage that is taxable, go to the IRS Website and search for the uniform premium table. To compare term life premium costs, measure them in cents per $1,000 dollars of monthly coverage. For an employee with a $35,000 life-insurance benefit, for example, if the monthly premium is $4.20, the cost is $0.12 per $1,000.

Accidental Death and Dismemberment (AD&D) insurance is usually an inexpensive add-on (rider) to the basic group-term-life policy. With AD&D coverage, an additional benefit is paid if death is caused by an accident or if the employee loses a limb, eye, or other body part. For a monthly two or three cents per $1,000 of coverage, AD&D can be a very inexpensive complement to the basic group life insurance coverage. Some insurance policies insist on inclusion of AD&D coverage for all employees with the group-term-life coverage.

Variations on basic group term insurance include, for example, business travel accident coverage, which provides a benefit if the employee is disabled, or if a dismemberment or death occurs while traveling on company business.

Disability insurance

Disability insurance provides for the replacement of pay when the employee is unable to work because of illness or disability. Unlike sick leave, disability insurance is administered by a third party that determines eligibility and the amount of payment. Although considered a "salary continuation" benefit, typically the benefits paid are less than the employee's salary. There are two general disability insurance plans: short-term and long-term, based on the length of coverage.

Both plans stipulate an "elimination period" during which the employee must be unable to work because of accident or disability. Also, both plans include a length-of-coverage clause that defines the longest period for which a covered employee will receive disability benefits. The extent of coverage defines the amount of benefit the employee is to receive. Typically, the coverage equals 66 percent of the employee's salary, up to a maximum amount per month.

Short-term disability insurance provides a regular income after a shorter elimination period (two weeks to one month), and it lasts for up to three or six months, depending on the policy selected. It typically costs employers more than long-term plans.

As an alternative to purchasing short-term disability insurance, some companies provide extended sick leave until the long-term disability insurance begins. Others allow employees to purchase their own short-term disability plans through payroll deduction. These plans often have very flexible characteristics (such as elimination period, length of coverage, and amount of coverage), so that an employee can select the plan best suited to his or her needs.

Long-term disability insurance provides a regular income after a longer elimination period and lasts for years. It is important to note whether the long-term disability policy the employer is considering provides coverage as long as the disabled employee is unable to work in his or her own occupation, or in any occupation. Many disability policies provide a benefit for only a year or two in the employee's own occupation, which will stop if the employee is able to work in *any* occupation. The most economical way for employers to provide long-term disability is to do so for all full-time employees.

It is important for businesses to dovetail their disability insurance plans with their sick leave policies to ensure that employees have continued salary replacement coverage. For example:

	Sick leave	S-T disability	L-T disability
	10 days accrued/yr	Begins two weeks after disability	Begins three months after disability
		Ends three months after disability	Ends at retirement age
Pay:	100 percent of days accrued	66 percent of regular pay	66 percent of regular pay

Retirement plans

Retirement and pension plans are offered through a wide variety of programs, from simple to complex. In the past, workers stayed with the same employer for their entire career, and "defined benefit" plans evolved. Funded by the employer, these plans promised workers a monthly pension upon retirement based on a formula that included annual wages, years of service, and age at retirement. The employer chose the investment vehicle, and contributions were based on actuarial valuation of the plan to ensure there would be sufficient funds for retirees.

With our more mobile workforce, in which both employers and careers change more frequently, "defined contribution" plans have become the most popular. These plans establish individual accounts for all participating employees. Employers can contribute to those accounts by matching employee contributions, although they are not required to do so. Usually, the employee can choose from among limited investment choices, but the plan's success depends on the amount invested and the financial success of the investments chosen. When the employee leaves the employer, he or she can usually "roll over" the funds to another qualified retirement plan such as an IRA, keeping them nontaxable until they are withdrawn after retirement.

Whenever an employer makes contributions under a retirement plan, the organization should consider the matter of vesting. Put simply, vesting is owning. If an employer's contributions immediately become 100-percent vested, those funds belong to the employee immediately. But if there is a vesting schedule (for example, retirement funds become vested once an employee has worked for the employer for a certain amount of time, such as five years), the employer's contribution will be returned to the organization if the employee is not vested.

How Vesting Works

Let's say an employer contributes matching funds of $1 for every $2 employees contribute to their retirement accounts, but the plan contains a five-year "cliff vesting" clause. An employee takes a job with a different employer. If he or she participated in the retirement plan for four and a half years, the employee did not meet the vesting requirement. Consequently, all of the employer's contributions go back to the employer. The employee keeps the remainder (his or her own contributions, plus any investment gain from the retirement plan).

Now let's say that another employer contributes the same match under its plan, but it has a graduated vesting schedule: 50 percent after three years of employment; 75 percent after four years; 100 percent after five years. Again, if the employee takes a job with another employer after four and a half (but less than five) years, he or she is 75-percent vested. Consequently, 25 percent of the employer's contributions go back to the employer, and the employee keeps the remainder.

For small employers, the most popular retirement plans are: 401(k), profit-sharing, savings incentive match plan for employees (SIMPLE), and simplified employee pension plan (SEP).

The Employee Retirement Income Security Act (ERISA) is the most significant legislation that affects retirement plans. By following its rules, employers and employees can take advantage of tax incentives, receive insurance protection covering retirement plans, and be assured of proper record-keeping and communications regarding their plans. Because of ERISA, retirement plans must pass a "fairness test" to ensure that they don't discriminate against lower-paid workers.

Discretionary benefits

Discretionary, or optional, benefits can supplement the provisions of core and government-mandated benefits. The more popular types of optional benefits follow.

Education assistance

Educational assistance provides tuition assistance primarily for courses at an accredited college or university, and occasionally for courses at trade schools or other entities. Reimbursement, which is usually dependent on a passing grade, may include all or a portion of the cost per credit hour, and the courses may or may not have to be directly related to the employee's job.

Transportation subsidies

Cover all or part of the cost for employees to take public transportation to and from work, participate in carpooling, or park their vehicles at or near work.

Add-on healthcare benefits

Many organizations' health insurance plans include, at little or no additional cost, a prescription drug discount plan and/or a vision care plan. Dental insurance is usually a stand-alone plan that includes basic preventive procedures (cleaning) and partial reimbursement for other procedures. Employee assistance programs (EAPs) provide confidential family and personal counseling services.

Flexible benefit plans

So-called Section 125 plans under the Internal Revenue Code (often referred to as "cafeteria plans") allow certain expenses to be paid out as payroll deductions before taxes are computed or deducted. The work to set up and administer these plans is directly related to how complex they are. In order, from the easiest to the most difficult for the employer there are:

✓ **Premium-only plans (POPs),** the most simple type of Section 125 plans, allow employees to pay their share of the premium for health and dental coverage with pretax dollars.

✓ **Flexible spending accounts,** combined with POPs, allow employees to use pretax dollars to pay for out-of-pocket health and care expenses that are not covered by insurance. Those can include eyeglasses, child care, prescription drugs, and other non-covered items. Flexible spending accounts are best administered by a third party for a monthly fee per participant. That method not only relieves staff of an exacting administrative chore so they can invest their energy elsewhere, it also ensures confidentiality and responsiveness to the participants.

✓ **Full cafeteria plans** are more popular in larger companies. Employees choose from a menu of eligible benefits by using credits the employer gives them at the beginning of the year. For example, an employee can choose to spend more pre-tax dollars on health insurance and less on disability insurance. Full cafeteria plans take careful thought to set up and considerable communication to explain to employee.

Work/life benefits

A growing trend in the benefits arena is to facilitate employees' achieving a balance between work and personal life. Indirectly, paid days off can add more time for vacation, and sick leave provisions allow using paid time off to care for an ill family member address the balancing act.

More directly, businesses are slowly adding new benefits that can affect employees' family life. Those benefits include childcare and elder care assistance, financial and health counseling programs, prepaid legal insurance, casual dress, flexible work options (such as telecommuting, job sharing, and compressed workweeks), group purchasing of auto and homeowners insurance, and on-site personal services (ATM, banking, travel, dry cleaners). Such non-traditional programs can contribute to employees' quality of life at work and at home.

For some employers, the benefits package is a cornerstone of the total compensation package. For others, benefits represent a nagging expense that keeps rising and rising. Overall, however, the importance of benefits can't be ignored: They represent 30 percent of employers' total compensation costs (the balance going to salaries and wages).[1]

Main message for managers

Some benefits are required by law, and others are provided voluntarily by organizations to bolster their strategies for competition in the marketplace and recruitment. Occasionally, benefits can be structured to encourage attendance and provide insurance coverage, inexpensively, that most employees could not afford otherwise.

With few exceptions, the cost of benefits has increased to become a sizable portion of employee remuneration. Healthcare benefits, for example, have risen far beyond the rate of inflation, prompting some employers to reduce or drop coverage and others to implement consumer-driven health plans that provide significant savings to both the employer and its employees.

Author

Michael Strand has 30 years of experience administering employee benefit plans and implementing and managing compensation programs. He consults for small and medium-sized companies, and is a licensed health- and life-insurance broker.

Chapter 7
Compensation

By Michael Strand

Not everything that can be counted counts, and not everything that counts can be counted.
—Attributed to Albert Einstein, awarded the Nobel Prize in Physics

Cash remuneration

Compensation can take many forms: pay, benefits, job satisfaction, camaraderie at work, opportunity for promotion, and many other variations. For this discussion, the word refers only to cash remuneration for work. That can include three components: base pay, incentives, and differentials.

Base pay is the salary or hourly wage. Incentives are designed to motivate workers to do more—more quickly, more accurately, and more cooperatively. Incentives often are paid as bonuses. Differentials are unique pay components related to work time or locations, or other less-desirable working conditions. For example, employers often apply a shift differential (such as 10 percent or $1.25 more per hour) for workers on evening or overnight shifts. Differentials are mostly industry-specific conventions, provided by organizations to be competitive with other organizations that do. The thrust of this chapter will be on base pay, with some commentary on incentives.

Employers are continuously striving to provide competitive pay without breaking the budget "bank." After all, for most organizations today, payroll is the major cost of business.

To decide what to pay their employees, organizations need a rational methodology, not a hit-and-miss or trial-and-error approach. What follows is a system for analyzing the job market and deriving a reasonably competitive compensation system.

Define the pay range

Sometimes referred to as market pricing, defining the pay range is based on the premise that all workers are being paid fairly. We know this is not completely true; some workers are paid more than their work is worth (notice we are not saying more than *the worker* is worth) because supply and demand are not balanced. Other workers are being paid less than their work is worth for discriminatory or traditional reasons. Through market pricing, organizations should define the worth of a position, then assess where a specific employee's pay should be on the pay range.

There are two bases on which to define the pay range: the average pay of all (or most) employees in that position, and the prevalent hiring rate for new employees in that position. With either method, the challenge is obtaining reliable information. Using the average rate provides better data that will help establish a more accurate pay range. Of the two types of averages, mean and median, the latter is best for salary comparisons because it represents the rate at which half of the salaries are higher and half are lower. Using the median rate minimizes a tendency for very high or very low salaries to skew the average.

The best source for finding the median rate for a given position is a published salary survey. Good ones have most of the following characteristics: a brief description of the position (sometimes containing typical qualifications such as education and experience); the mean, median, 25th percentile, and 75th percentile; data grouped by organization size (number of employees or annual revenues); geographic location; type of organization; effective date of the data; and list of participating organizations.

Average pay information is available on the Internet, but be careful: If the data does not reflect your organization's profile, it is probably unreliable. Online market data for sale will probably be more reliable than free data, but there are no guarantees, which brings us back to published salary surveys. WorldatWork publishes the *Survey Handbook & Directory*, which contains many articles on the use of surveys and survey data, as well as a list of hundreds of published surveys according to type and region.[1]

The Society for Human Resource Management (SHRM) provides its members with listings of available surveys by industry and job category, including free Websites and free data.

Purchasing salary surveys can be expensive. Once you have identified two or three surveys applicable to your positions, it's a good idea to participate with the firms that conduct those surveys by providing your own organization's data to them. These companies rely on participants to provide reliable results and usually grant a significant discount when you buy their published reports. (Some will give you a discount on a current survey if you agree to provide data for their next survey.)

Be aware that conducting your own salary survey may be illegal. Court cases in the early 1990s led the U.S. Department of Justice and the Federal Trade Commission to conclude that salary surveys may violate antitrust laws. Consequently, they created an "antitrust safety zone" for such surveys. Among its requirements are that the survey is managed by an independent third party, the data is more than three months old, and at least five participating organizations are reporting data for the survey. Most important, the survey cannot allow participants to identify the compensation paid by a specific organization.

If the survey data is more than six months old consider raising it by a few percentage points to accommodate the general market trend to increase salaries.

Let's create a hypothetical example. Here is a sample worksheet with the data averages you have gathered from one or more salary surveys:

Administrative Assistant		
Profile match	Mean	Median
Revenues ($1 to $2.5 million)	$31.5	$30.8
Size (under 25 employees)	$32.1	$31.7
Organization type (financial)	$33.4	$33.5
Location (your city or region)	$33.1	$30.9
Market rate		$31.7

You have gathered the survey averages that best match your organization. You decide to give all four profile characteristics equal weight. The result (an average of the four median rates) is the market rate for the administrative assistant position, $31,725 (not rounded as in the worksheet). Based on these assumptions, half the administrative assistants in other surveyed organizations in your market and with your employer's profile are paid more than $31,725, and half are paid less.

A pay range defines the maximum and minimum for the position. The range spread is the maximum minus the minimum and then divided by the minimum. To create a pay range from this market rate, know the HR practices regarding range spreads for different levels of positions: For entry-level and support positions, the range spread is usually minimal, from 35 percent to 40 percent; for professional positions, from 50 percent to 60 percent. The range spread for supervisory and managerial positions is from 60 percent to 70 percent, and for vice president/executive positions, from 70 percent to 80 percent.

The following table will help us create the pay range.

Pay Range Development Factors		
35% = 1.149	50% = 1.2	65% = 1.245
40% = 1.1666	55% = 1.2155	70% = 1.26
45% = 1.1833	60% = 1.231	75% = 1.2735

We pick the slightly wider range spread of 40 percent for this support position. To define the range, refer to the following steps.

1. Identify the range midpoint or market rate: $31,725.

2. Multiply the midpoint ($31,725) by the pay range factor. In this example we want a 40-percent range, so the factor is 1.1666. Thus, $31,725 × 1.1666 = $37,010.4 = range maximum. Round this amount down to $37,010.

3. Subtract the range midpoint ($31,725) from the range maximum ($37,010) = $5,285. Subtract that difference ($5,285) from the range midpoint ($31,725) = $26,440 = range minimum.

4. Add the midpoint ($31,725) to the minimum ($26,440), then divide by 2 = $29,082 = top of the first quartile.

5. Add the midpoint ($31,725) to the maximum ($37,010), then divide by 2 = $34,417 = top of the third quartile.

Minumum	1st Quartile	Midpoint	3rd Quartile	Maximum
3	4	1	5	2
$26,440	$29,082	$31,725	$34,417	$37,010

Now we have defined the pay range with all the important benchmarks. This range represents the marketplace for the administrative assistant position. It is an appropriate range if you want to meet the going rate. But if you want to exceed the market rate, adjust it to a new market rate between the midpoint and the third quartile (for example, $33,071) and recalculate the range following the previous steps.

Using the pay range

To use the pay range effectively, we need to know what level(s) of in-position experience relate to the range benchmarks. Some (too few) salary surveys provide an average time in position for the individual employees. If we knew that the average time in position for the surveyed administrative assistants was 4.5 years, we could place that comparable experience level at the midpoint ($31,725). We could then use the following guidelines to help us determine a salary offer for a job candidate.

The organization could expect to pay that midpoint ($31,725) or more to a candidate with at least 4.5 years of direct experience at the same or greater level of responsibility.

For job candidates with less direct experience, a lower offer would be more appropriate:

✓ For a candidate with little or no direct experience at the same level of responsibility, offer closer to the minimum of the range—between $26,440 and half-way to the midpoint (that is, the first quartile): $29,082.

✓ For a candidate with two to four years direct experience at the same level of responsibility, offer between $29,082 and the midpoint of $31,725.

Although there is no assurance that the candidate will accept an offer within these guidelines, they provide a starting point for negotiation.

The midpoint, or market rate, is the median; that is, half the administrative assistants in your market earn more and half earn less. Presumably, those in the first half have more experience than the others. So unless particular circumstances indicate otherwise, there is no rational reason for an organization to offer an "experienced-level" pay rate to a candidate who does not have at least the average amount of experience. It is also important to differentiate between applicable experience (building up to administrative assistant) and comparable experience (equal to the position).

Benchmarking positions

You probably will not find salary-survey data for all your positions. Ideally, you will have data on half of them, so you can use those positions for which you have derived market rates as your "benchmark" positions. These positions become points in your organizational hierarchy from which you can assign market rates and midpoints for other positions. Here's an example of how it works:

Your market rate for an administrative assistant is $31,725. Through the surveys, you also have a market rate for a staff accountant: $38,150. But you have no salary data for widget technician, although you believe (based on qualifications, contributions to the organization's mission, and so forth) it should fall between administrative assistant and staff accountant. Create a table similar to this:

Benchmark Positions	Assigned Positions	Market Rate	Assigned Market Rate
Staff Accountant		$38,150	
	Widget Technician		?
Administrative Assistant		$31,725	

Based on your understanding of the three jobs, should the widget technician earn an amount halfway between the two benchmark positions—$34,937? Or should the technician's pay be closer to the staff accountant's market rate—say, $36,543? If you are unsure, work up the pay range for both scenarios and look at the salary of the widget technician to see whether its placement on the ranges makes more sense under one circumstance than another.

Pay ranges and formal grades

As we have seen, developing pay ranges can be very helpful in determining salary offers for new hires and assessing employees' pay relative to the marketplace. But the decision whether or not to have formal grades based on those ranges varies among organizations. Generally, larger organizations tend to have a formal grade structure; many smaller organizations administer an effective compensation system without formal grades.

Communicating about pay

Communicating pay decisions can pose a significant challenge: How much is communicated, how much is withheld, and how much of the decision-making process is revealed are judgments to be made by the organization's leaders.

According to WorldatWork's *Market Pricing*, "Pay delivers a strong message. No other area is more important to employees in their relationship with their company. ... [T]he most financially successful companies are more likely to communicate pay information to their employees... ."[2]

At the other extreme is this philosophy, from a switching supervisor at a long-distance-telephone firm: "We know that communication is a problem, but the company is not going to discuss it with the employees."

The right approach to communicating depends on the organization's management style and corporate culture, as well as on employee perceptions. Here are some questions that can guide organization to create a communication plan that makes sense.

What compensation information is communicated?

Following is a menu of communication information that your organization may or may not want to communicate to employees and appropriate supervisors.

✓ *Individual employee pay change.* Communicate each employee pay increase first to the supervisor and then to the affected employee, along with the reason for the increase. Example: "market adjustment," with an explanation such as, "Effective _____ [date], you will receive an increase in your pay from $XX.xx to $YY.yy. This increase will be a market adjustment based on our recent compensation study."

✓ *Pay grade/range.* If you have a formal pay structure, communicate employees' pay grades or ranges individually. The pay grade, of course, identifies the range minimum and maximum and other benchmarks. Communicating the pay range, however, begs the question, "What happens when my pay reaches the maximum for my range?" Typically, the pay range should increase each year as the pay rates in the job market increase. However, the organization should develop an above-maximum (or "red circle") policy for employees whose pay rate is above the maximum for their range.

Is their pay frozen until the position's pay range maximum increases to an amount above their pay? Are they eligible for bonuses only? Are the usual merit or general increases paid in the form of a bonus (one-time payment), thereby not increasing their base pay rate? Are they treated the same as all other employees—receiving full merit and market base pay increases—the first year they are red-circled?

✓ *Salary schedule.* Many organizations publish their complete pay-range schedule (excluding position titles) for all employees to see, reasoning that employees can easily share each other's pay ranges anyway, so why keep it secret?

✓ *A position's market rate.* Sharing the position's market rate with an employee can be an effective retention tool. It informs the employee of what his or her position pays compared with peers in the marketplace. However, similar to other compensation information, it may be challenged by employees ("How did you determine this rate?"). Most organizations share the market rate with appropriate supervisory-level employees.

To whom is compensation information communicated?

Timeliness and consistency of message will be key in ensuring that proper communication occurs. For consistency, it is hard to beat communicating the message on paper.

Larger organizations (more than 100 employees) could decide to share more compensation information with managers and coordinators, and rely on them to communicate it to their staffs. However, the risk of delegating communication this way is that not all information is likely to be communicated consistently.

The executive or management team is often involved in reviewing expected pay changes before a final decision is made. Any verbal discussion with employees should supplement written documentation to keep executive staff in the communication loop.

What is communicated?

Minimally, a memorandum to each employee should identify his or her current rate, the new rate, the effective date of the increase, and which pay period will reflect the increase. Additionally, it should give the reason(s) for the new rate such as overall adjustment, merit increase, market adjustment, or equity adjustment.

When does the communication take place?

Compensation communication generally occurs in two stages: First, to affected executives, managers, and coordinators to obtain feedback, anticipate employee reaction, and make adjustments if necessary. Second, written and verbal communication to employees directly or through their supervisors.

Incentive pay

Incentive pay is intended to motivate employees by paying for performance that exceeds expectations. Incentives can be structured to address short-term achievements or long-term results. There are three major types of incentives: individual, group, and organization-wide.

Individual incentives may be commissions earned by salespeople or a piece-rate system that measures productivity in a manufacturing plant. In an office environment, incentives may take the form of cash bonuses. Whatever the form, provide the reward as soon after the achievement as possible.

Group incentives can be used when it is impractical to assess individuals' contributions. A popular form of group incentive is gainsharing, in which the group and the organization share, through a cash bonus, the benefits of the group's productivity above and beyond the standard established.

Organization-wide incentives can include profit-sharing and stock ownership. Exceeding the organization's financial goals may result in bonus payments for all employees. The form of the payment may be flat dollar or a percentage of base pay.

A solid compensation structure is founded on understanding the organization's positions (job descriptions), identifying the pay for other positions in the marketplace (salary surveys), using survey data to develop pay ranges (compensation methodology), and using the pay ranges to guide supervisors in hiring practices and managing the pay (performance evaluation and pay-for-performance) of employees.

Main message for managers

There are several ways to compensate employees, but the most important of all is fairly. In larger organizations, salary ranges, pay grades, and other types of remuneration for work performed are usually set by top management, with input from senior staff and the finance and human resources departments. If your organization doesn't have such a pay plan, you might be charged with creating one for your team. That takes research and arithmetic, not just what "seems" fair.

Good managerial judgment trumps past practices every time: You may have to re-address past disparities or determine pay for a newly created position, or even defend the reasons for a raise or bonus. But even without an existing template, creating one is easier than you think: Managers and HR professionals can use existing resources to set up a workable and fair compensation plan.

Author

Michael Strand has 30 years experience administering employee benefit plans and implementing and managing compensation programs. He consults for small and medium-sized companies, and is a licensed health- and life-insurance broker.

Chapter 8
Employee
Relations

Write people's accomplishments in stone, and their faults in sand.

—Benjamin Franklin, American statesman, scientist, philosopher, author, and inventor

Maintaining an office environment that is conducive to work is the foundation of a good employee-relations program.

The manager's philosophy

Managers can choose to treat employees in a respectful way or not. However, going the respect route is an HR "best practice" that can yield higher levels of productivity and lower turnover. Plus, it's the right thing to do.

If you really respect your employees, you'll want to make sure that each one has current, realistic performance objectives and a clear understanding of his or her job responsibilities. To do that effectively, you'll want to improve your skills as a coach and counselor so you can help employees succeed.

Remember that your own success as a manager depends upon your ability to get things done and reach your goals through your employees. At the same time, you need to lead, support, and develop your team members, which can be a tough balancing act. Let's distinguish between a coach and a counselor, then explore how to help employees make a significant contribution to your company.

Coach vs. counselor

As a *coach*, a manager identifies an employee's need for instruction and direction; the need is usually directly related to his or her performance or career goals. Coaching is a collaborative approach to improving job-related performance; It relies on mutual, progressive goal-setting, personal feedback, and an ongoing, supportive relationship.

Most managers coach because it helps retain employees, shows that they care about their employees as individuals, and builds stronger working relationships.

Managers should be ready to coach when a problem occurs, a new procedure is introduced, a job is changed, and/or a skill gap is identified.

As a *counselor*, a manager first identifies a problem that interferes with an employee's work performance. In such situations, the manager needs to switch from coaching to counseling mode. Think of this as a process that helps the employee define specifically what behavior he or she needs to change in order to improve his or her performance or resolve a problem.

The manager's goal is to be *both* a good coach and a good counselor, and he or she must have the sensitivity to know which mode to use and when. Generally, coaching should precede counseling.

A good manager who is both a coach and a counselor:

✓ Motivates employees to do good work.

✓ Reinforces good performance.

✓ Encourages employees to stretch.

✓ Sets clear expectations.

✓ Provides positive feedback on an ongoing basis; provides constructive feedback on a timely basis.

✓ Acknowledges employees' progress toward their goals.

Mantra and models

The manager's mantra consists of six simple words: *When you see it, say it!*

That should serve as a constant reminder that you need to be communicating with your employees all the time. Make a habit of giving performance feedback on a frequent, scheduled basis. This includes not only corrective but also positive feedback.

Mark Twain said, "I can live for two months on a good compliment." Managers have to remember to beat his time and address problematic behavior as soon as they notice it.

To make this concept easier to remember, think of two acronyms:

Positive Feedback	Corrective Feedback
F = **F**requent	**B** = **B**ehavior
A = **A**ccurate	**E** = **E**ffect
S = **S**pecific	**E** = **E**xpectation
T = **T**imely	**R** = **R**esults

Because corrective feedback can be a bit more difficult, let's consider the following example.

Richard is a customer service specialist who handles phone calls from corporate customers who have questions about data and computer networks. His manager monitored seven of Richard's phone calls today, and, in four of them, the manager heard him chatting with a coworker while a customer was on the phone. Richard's behavior is unprofessional, it compromises the company's service to customers, it could cost the company a valuable customer, and it distracts other staff working nearby. Richard is expected to focus on the customer and provide stellar service, without exception. He should use his breaks to socialize with colleagues. His manager needs to have a serious conversation with him.

Here's how the manager could give corrective feedback.

Behavior: "Richard, I monitored your calls today and heard you talking with coworkers while customers were on the line—on four different calls."

Effect: "This behavior could cost us customers, and it distracts other employees."

Expectation: "As you know, you're expected to focus on the customer exclusively and have no side conversations."

Result: "You can turn this around. You have the ability to be one of our best customer service representatives if you save your socializing for break time. And I'll be one of your biggest supporters."

A Closer Look

Why was Richard talking to coworkers when he was supposed to be helping customers? Perhaps he isn't aware of how important his role is in retaining customers. Perhaps his friends at work are a competing priority, more important to him than doing a good job, minding his phone manners, or providing good customer service.

Other possible competing priorities are personal issues, health problems, or conflicting job demands. An employee who isn't meeting performance expectations might say that he doesn't know how, or isn't provided with the resources needed, to perform a certain task. Perhaps he just doesn't *want* to focus on the customer. This is definitely something his manager should explore.

Many symptoms can indicate performance problems, including:

✓ Decreased productivity.

✓ Poor quality work.

✓ Missed due dates.

✓ Avoidance of tougher tasks.

✓ Disorganization.

✓ Leaning on others.

✓ Being away from desk for long periods.

✓ Upward delegation.

✓ Little or no initiative.

✓ Increased complaining.

✓ Lack of cooperation.

✓ Blaming failure on others.

✓ Lack of enthusiasm.

Poor performance can affect your department in several ways:

✓ Decreased productivity.

✓ Decreased morale.

✓ Customer dissatisfaction.

✓ Increased stress.

✓ Decreased efficiency.

✓ Increased cost.

Clearly, unsatisfactory performance must be identified and corrected on a timely basis.

It benefits us, as managers, to create the type of work environment and communication needed to minimize performance problems.

But sometimes, despite our good efforts to correct poor performance, issues remain.

Progressive discipline

Effective managers bring a positive attitude and a supportive tone to dealing with performance problems. Supervisors want their employees to succeed, and they recognize their role in that process. It is in everyone's interest to develop a successful employment relationship.

When an employee has work problems, a manager must initially step back and ask why the behavior is not meeting expectations. Is it important to discuss? Was the employee aware of what was expected? Did you, as the manager, offer the employee tangible support in meeting an expectation?

If you have made every effort to help the employee, yet significant problems still exist, you must address the situation quickly and firmly, usually following a specific sequence.

Progressive discipline is the manager's effort to be fair and equitable. It provides several opportunities for the employee to improve. But discipline should be initiated only after ensuring that the problem has been investigated (and determined to be legitimate) and sufficiently documented.

Disciplinary options include:

✓ Informal discussion.

✓ Verbal warning.

✓ Written warning.

✓ Final warning.

✓ Termination.

Before taking these steps, the manager should prepare a complete chronology of specific facts and events. In the initial discussion, the manager should guide the employee to agree that a problem exists. The manager should go over the facts while giving the employee an opportunity to respond or explain. Together, they should plan a remedial course of action in detail—outlining what needs to be done and setting dates for when changes must be made. It's critical for the manager to offer genuine assistance or training, if appropriate, to help the employee succeed. The manager conscientiously monitors the situation, and should acknowledge and reinforce improvement as it occurs.

Once the employee has met expectations, recognize his or her success. If the employee has not done so, review your documentation with the HR department or legal counsel to prepare for termination of employment.

Checklist for discussions

✓ Make it private and productive. Arrange a time and a place where you won't be distracted or interrupted.

✓ Create a comfortable and problem-solving atmosphere.

✓ State your purpose clearly:

   ✏ Give your perception of performance against agreed-upon standards.

   ✏ Explore possible contributing factors.

   ✏ Describe what you want, need, or expect from the employee.

✓ Check the employee's understanding of what's expected.

   ✏ Ask for, and listen to, the employee's point of view.

   ✏ Ask questions to understand the context of the actions or behavior at issue.

✓ Identify what changes are needed.

   ✏ Agree on a timetable and a method of measurement.

   ✏ Communicate clearly what happens next if the problem is not resolved.

   ✏ Express support and encouragement.

   ✏ Set up a method for monitoring the employee's progress.

Documentation

To prepare for difficult conversations, managers must make notes as a habit, including both negative and positive performance. Good performance management entails creating a clear, accurate written memo, shared with the employee, that objectively captures the performance issues and the commitments made during the conversation.

Sample Memorandum of Warning

Confidential Memorandum

Date: [Current date]
To: [Employee]
From: [Supervisor, title]
Subject: Performance Concerns

As we discussed during our meeting on [date], I am concerned about your job performance. Specifically, I have concerns about the poor quality of many of your work products, including written memos and reports. These written products, as I showed you, often contain many grammatical errors, misspellings, and typographical errors.

One of your responsibilities as a [job title] is to be able to "review and proofread outgoing correspondence, checking for proper format, grammar, and punctuation." Some of the examples I shared with you during our conversation included:

-
-
-

As a [job title], you are also expected to perform most of your duties without immediate supervisory oversight. In too many instances, I feel I have to provide more guidance than I give others in order to get our department's work completed. A recent example of this was [include specific details].

One of the key factors in our performance appraisal form is quality of work. This factor is critical to your achieving each of the objectives we set together at the beginning of our performance cycle and reconfirmed in our meeting [date]. At this time, the quality of your work is below the acceptable standards we set during the same meeting at the beginning of our performance cycle.

To help you improve the quality of your work, I will meet with you weekly for the next 60 days. During this time, I will review most of your written work with you. If you need assistance or have questions in between our meetings, I will help you. However, I expect you to work toward completing routine work on time and correctly—the first time.

Please review this memo carefully; it is intended as a corrective action. I expect to see substantial and sustained improvement both during and after the 60-day period and, if at any time I do not see that level of improvement, we will have more serious conversations, up to and including a termination discussion.

Please let me know how else I can help you improve in these areas and whether you have any questions about this memo.

I have read and understand this warning and have had the opportunity to discuss it with my supervisor.

_____

Name   Date

Tips for Effective Documentation

✓ *Do not use emotionally charged words.*
✓ *Focus on the performance or behavior, not the employee.*
✓ *Be objective and clear.*
✓ *Clarify performance expectations and the consequences of failure to improve.*
✓ *Make notes on meetings immediately afterward.*
✓ *Keep the notes confidential (share only with those who have a need to know).*

Termination

"Termination" of employment technically includes both resigning (voluntary) and being laid off or fired (involuntary). When the employer decides on the latter, it's often because of poor performance, misconduct, or changed business needs that require eliminating or restructuring positions. Cases of egregious conduct may subject an employee to immediate termination.

Finally, if the poor performance, insubordination, or failure to follow company policy is not corrected following the last appropriate warning—or there is a relapse after progressive discipline—a manager should consider termination.

Termination is one of the most difficult parts of a manager's job, and the message is one of the hardest for an employee to hear.

Regardless of the reason for a termination, managers should always deliver the news in a sensitive and humane way—and not until they are sure that termination is the appropriate step.

Before deciding to terminate an employee, consider the following questions:

✓ Would you take the same step for any employee in this situation?

✓ Is this a lawful, non-discriminatory reason for termination?

✓ Have your supervisor(s) or top executives reviewed and approved your decision to terminate?

✓ Will you be able to explain the termination decision to the employee clearly and honestly?

✓ Will you be able to explain the termination to the employee's colleagues?

Once the decision is made, use the following step-by-step procedures.

How to Conduct a Termination

Before the meeting

✓ *Prepare a "recommendation to terminate" memo and obtain appropriate approvals.*

✓ *Decide on the amount of severance, if appropriate.*

✓ *Notify colleagues who have a need to know.*

✓ *Schedule a private place for the meeting.*

✓ *Prepare talking points for the meeting.*

✓ *Check your state's law to determine whether the meeting needs to include giving the employee a hand-cut check for hours worked since the most recent paycheck.*

✓ *Invite a representative from the HR or legal department to sit in, or—if those departments don't exist at your company—invite another senior manager.*

It is wise to anticipate a range of reactions from the employee who is being terminated. Remain calm and clear; it can be devastating news.

During the meeting

✓ Briefly explain the termination decision to the employee. Review progressive disciplinary steps and other measures the company has taken to help the employee. Be direct and to the point.

✓ Give the employee an opportunity to react and respond.

✓ Clarify that the decision is irreversible and that upper levels of management agree with the decision.

✓ Collect all company property from the employee (such as keys, IDs, passes, or laptops).

✓ Remind the employee of the company policy regarding references, if one exists.

✓ Explain the right to apply for unemployment.

✓ Discuss health insurance, the employee's final paycheck, payment for unused vacation, and, if appropriate, severance pay.

✓ Inform the employee in person or by providing a letter stating that he or she will receive information regarding benefits, wages, insurance, pension or rollover, and the like by mail.

✓ Get a forwarding address.

✓ Get signature(s) on confidentiality agreements and other applicable forms.

✓ Explain when and how the employee should exit the building.

✓ Explain the policy regarding future access to the office.

✓ Tell the employee that this is a confidential process and will be shared with only those who have a legitimate need to know.

✓ Discuss how you will notify coworkers.

✓ Escort the employee to his or her office or desk area while he or she is gathering personal belongings, or offer to pack and mail them. If possible, minimize the number of employees who might be nearby during this step.

✓ Throughout the process, always allow the employee to retain his or her dignity.

After the meeting

✓ Share the employee's departure with the work group in the agreed-upon manner; be sensitive and concise.

✓ Notify appropriate internal staff and any customers, vendors, or other external people affected by the employee's leaving.

✓ Write a summary of the termination meeting. Have the witnesses (HR/legal/other manager present) sign and date that document.

✓ Send checks to terminated employee (or make sure that finance or HR does so).

✓ Follow up on any other commitments to the employee.

✓ Determine who will take over the employee's responsibilities and, if that person is on staff, discuss the work with him or her.

Termination don'ts

✓ *Don't make the meeting long.*

✓ *Don't go on the defensive.*

✓ *Don't be insensitive.*

✓ *Don't use humor.*

✓ *Don't make promises you can't keep.*

Main message for managers

Frequent, specific, accurate, and timely feedback is one of the most critical requirements for sustained high-level performance. Without it, performance may fail.

When performance issues exist, treat the employee as an adult and provide genuine support for him or her to change.

> Flatter me and I may not believe you.
>
> Criticize me and I may not like you.
>
> Ignore me and I may not forgive you.
>
> Encourage me and I will not forget you.

—William Arthur Ward, author of *Fountains of Faith*

Chapter 9
Legal
Considerations

By Joyce L. Oliner, Esq.

It is the spirit and not the form of law that keeps justice alive.

—Earl Warren

Notice

This chapter summarizes some of the key employment law issues for managers and HR staff. Every employment situation is different, however, and may be covered by a variety of federal, state, and local laws that are beyond the scope of this overview. This chapter therefore is not intended to be, and should not be used as, a substitute for specific legal advice.

The U.S. workplace is subject to a host of laws aimed at protecting employees. But the prospect of a legal issue need not paralyze managers. Armed with an understanding of the legal framework governing HR, managers can achieve their operational goals with minimal legal risk.

Employment at will

Most managers have heard of "employment at will," but many aren't sure what it means. First, the good news: The legal concept of employment at will is alive and well in virtually every state, meaning that an employer can terminate the employment of an employee at any time and for any reason, just as the employee can resign at any time and for any reason. Now the bad news: The employer may not exercise its right to terminate employment "at will" for an *unlawful* reason. Although employment at will functions as the bedrock of employment law, it is subject to so many legal limitations that it often fails to help managers navigate an employment law problem.

Instead, managers need broad familiarity with the legal concepts they are most likely to encounter in managing employees. Here, we'll review the principal legal issues managers should bear in mind during the three stages of employment status: hiring, on-the-job, and termination.

Hiring

Equal Employment Opportunity (EEO) laws aim to provide equal employment opportunity to all workers by barring certain specific forms of discrimination against employees and applicants for employment. Retaliation against employees who assert their rights under these laws, or who assist others to do so, is illegal.

The three federal EEO statutes with which managers should be most familiar are:

✓ Title VII of the Civil Rights Act of 1964 (Title VII), which applies to employers of 15 employees or more, and prohibits an employer from discriminating based on race, color, gender, national origin, or religion.

✓ The Americans with Disabilities Act of 1990 (ADA), which also applies to employers of 15 or more, bars discrimination because of a person's physical or mental disability, and it requires the employer to provide reasonable accommodations to disabled individuals during the hiring process and during employment. The ADA protects those who are actually disabled, those who have a record of a disability, and those whom the employer regards as disabled.

✓ The Age Discrimination in Employment Act of 1967 (ADEA), which applies to employers of 20 or more, prohibits discrimination based on age against employees age 40 or over in favor of younger ones. There is no upper age limit, except in very narrowly defined circumstances, so mandatory retirement is illegal in most cases.

BFOQs

In very limited situations, EEO law recognizes that certain protected characteristics may be "bona fide occupational qualifications" that an employer can legally consider. For example:

✓ *A theater hiring performers for female roles may exclude male applicants from consideration.*

✓ *A religious institution may require that its clergy share the religious beliefs of the hiring institution.*

These BFOQ exceptions are very narrow and unlikely to apply in a typical workplace. Race can never be a BFOQ.

Do's and don'ts of pre-offer questions

✓ In job advertisements or other recruiting materials don't state a preference for applicants of a particular age, race, gender, or other legally protected characteristic.

✓ Don't engage in discriminatory hiring to try to please your customers; customer preference is never a defense to a charge of employment discrimination.

✓ Don't ask questions in employment applications or interviews that will give you information you would be legally barred from using, such as an applicant's age or national origin.

✓ Remember that the ADA imposes very strict limitations on the medical inquiries you can make during the hiring process. Before you offer a job, you can't ask questions that would tend to disclose the existence of a disability. Examples of *prohibited* pre-offer questions include:

  ☞ How many sick days did you take at your last job?

  ☞ Have you ever filed a workers' compensation claim?

  ☞ What medications are you currently taking?

✓ Examples of *permissible* pre-offer questions:

  ☞ Can you perform this job, with or without reasonable accommodation?

  ☞ Do you need a reasonable accommodation to perform this job? (Ask this only if you reasonably believe the candidate has a disability that would interfere with his or her job performance.)

Drug tests are not considered medical exams for ADA purposes, and can be required (subject to applicable state laws) before or after the employer offers the job.

The best way to avoid EEO problems during the hiring process is to make hiring decisions based on the requirements of the position you are trying to fill, not on stereotypical assumptions about certain groups of people. For example, don't exclude the mother of young children on the assumption that she will be less willing to work long hours. However, feel free to look elsewhere if she tells you during the interview that she must leave work daily at 4 p.m. to collect her children from daycare. That's a legitimate business decision based on fact, not on an assumption.

Negligent hiring

To avoid this state-law claim, you must take reasonable care when hiring employees. At the least, you should:

✓ Closely review documents the applicant has submitted to find any gaps or inconsistencies that the he or she needs to explain.

✓ Always check references, even if all you learn is "name, rank, and serial number." At least you've confirmed that the applicant stated his or her work history correctly.

Contract issues

We all recognize that, if the employer and the new hire sign a written document titled "Employment Contract," the parties will be bound to honor the promises in it. But managers often forget that there are other ways employers can create legally binding contractual obligations. Your statements during the interview can come back to haunt you. If you say, "You'll be a VP by next spring if you take this job," the applicant can take the statement as a promise, and a reason to pass up other job offers. If the position does not materialize as promised, the angry employee may file a claim for breach of contract. Statements made in offer letters can also be construed as contractually binding.

To minimize the risk of inadvertently creating contractual rights, you should:

✓ Understand that what you say, verbally or in writing, to an applicant may be viewed as contractually binding, and steer clear of statements that could appear to be guarantees of long tenure, particular disciplinary processes, or career paths, unless you're sure your organization will be able to make good on those promises.

✓ Include in your employment application form, offer letter, and employee manual a statement that employment is at will, and that the at-will nature of employment can be altered only by a specific written document signed by the CEO or other senior executive.

Background checks

If you are using a third-party service (such as a credit reporting agency) to obtain credit reports, criminal or driving records, or other background information as part of your hiring process, you must comply with the detailed notice and consent requirements of the Fair Credit Reporting Act (FCRA), as well as with any applicable state laws. The FCRA has additional requirements if you plan to deny employment based entirely or partly on the results of the background check. For more information, check the Federal Trade Commission's Website (*www.ftc.gov/bcp/conline/pubs/buspubs/credempl.shtm*).

In addition to the federal requirements under the FCRA, many state laws limit how employers can use criminal records. Generally, using arrest record information is prohibited, and conviction information can be used only if it is material to the position being filled.

Immigration

The Immigration Reform and Control Act (IRCA) requires employers to verify all new employees' identity and eligibility to work via Form I-9 within three business days of hire. The form is available at the Website of the federal Citizenship and Immigration Services (*www.uscis.gov/files/form/i-9.pdf*).

Some points to remember:

- ✓ Everyone must complete a Form I-9, whether they were born in the United States or not.
- ✓ Form I-9 prescribes which forms of documentation are acceptable; the employer can't require the new hire to produce more or different documents.
- ✓ If the documents the new hire presents appear genuine, the employer must accept them.

On the job

Remember that the EEO laws ban discrimination in all terms and conditions of employment, including compensation, training, assignments, disciplinary action, and layoffs.

EEO and independent contractors

Title VII, the ADA, the ADEA, and most state EEO laws protect employees and job applicants, not independent contractors. Unfortunately, the legal line between employees and contractors is not always clear, and employers sometimes find themselves sued for EEO violations by "contractors" claiming to be employees. Consult your legal counsel for advice about the correct classification of your workers.

Harassment

The prohibition against discrimination also bans harassment based on a legally protected characteristic. Illegal harassment is defined as unwelcome conduct based on a protected characteristic if:

✓ Enduring the offensive conduct becomes a condition of continued employment.

✓ The conduct is severe or pervasive enough to create a work environment that a reasonable person would consider intimidating, hostile, or abusive.

Some examples of harassing behavior include making fun of an employee's religious beliefs or referring to foreign-born employees using derogatory stereotypes. The harasser can be the victim's supervisor or coworker, client, vendor, or other non-employee. The victim does not have to be the person directly harassed, but can be anyone affected by the offensive conduct.

The "work environment" is defined broadly for these purposes: It includes not only the employer's premises during work hours, but also wherever and whenever the employee is working for the employer, such as at a client's site, a trade show, or a conference. Even some work-related social events, such as the employer's annual holiday party, may be deemed the work environment.

The most familiar type of harassment is sexual harassment, which includes acts such as touching a coworker inappropriately, engaging in derogatory stereotyping about one gender, telling obscene jokes, displaying pornographic images, or offering job advantages in return for sexual favors. The victim can be a man or a woman, and the harasser doesn't have to be of the opposite sex for the conduct to be illegal.

As a manager, what can you do to minimize the risk of unlawful harassment in your workplace?

✓ Be a positive role model: Avoid engaging in conduct that could reasonably be viewed as harassing.

✓ Address inappropriate behavior even before it rises to the level of illegality.

✓ Make sure your organization has a clear written policy prohibiting all types of workplace harassment, and establish a confidential complaint procedure for employees to report suspected harassment.

✓ Train both supervisors and nonsupervisors about harassment prevention as part of new-hire orientation, and provide refresher courses periodically.

✓ If you receive a complaint of harassment or otherwise become aware of it, move promptly to investigate and, if you decide that the behavior described in the complaint really was harassment or other inappropriate conduct, take action to remedy the problem immediately.

✓ Handle any harassment investigation with care and discretion to avoid legal claims from not only the complaining employee but also the accused harasser.

✓ Ensure that employees who make complaints of harassment in good faith do not suffer retaliation.

Protections for sick or disabled employees

A variety of legal rights apply to sick or disabled employees, starting with their entitlement to time off (leave).

The main federal leave law is the Family and Medical Leave Act (FMLA). It applies only to employers with at least 50 employees. To be entitled to FMLA leave, the employee must:

✓ Have been employed by the employer for at least 12 months.

✓ Have worked at least 1,250 hours during the 12 months preceding the leave.

✓ Work at a location where there are 50 or more employees within a 75-mile radius.

State leave laws

Many states have enacted their own leave statutes, addressing time off for illness, pregnancy, childbirth, and family care. State workers' compensation laws may also cover employees injured on the job. Check your state's laws to determine which rules apply to your employees.

The FMLA entitles eligible employees to take 12 weeks of unpaid leave in any 12-month period for any of these reasons:

✓ His or her own serious health condition.

✓ Caring for a spouse, parent, or child with a serious health condition.

✓ The birth of a child to the employee.

✓ Fostering or adopting a child.

An employee may choose, or the employer may require the employee, to substitute accrued paid vacation, personal leave, or sick leave during this period. Also, leave covered by workers' compensation may count against the employee's FMLA entitlement.

The definition of a "serious health condition" is complex, and it is not the same as a disability under the ADA. An ADA disability typically involves a long-term condition, but a serious health condition can be as temporary as the flu, provided that the employee has been unable to work for three consecutive days, has seen a healthcare provider, and has been prescribed medication. For more information, check the U.S. Department of Labor's Website (*www.dol.gov/elaws/esa/fmla/shc.asp*).

Some FMLA do's and don'ts:

✓ Do include an FMLA policy in your employee handbook, and post an FMLA notice in your workplace (available at *www.dol.gov/esa/regs/compliance/posters/fmla.htm*).

✓ Do provide employees taking FMLA leave with written notice, within two business days, that their leave will be counted as FMLA leave.

✓ Do reinstate employees returning within the FMLA leave period to their old positions or virtually identical ones, unless the employee would have lost his or her job regardless of the leave, such as in a reduction in force.

✓ Don't retaliate against employees for taking FMLA leave (including a negative performance review because the employee missed time while on FMLA leave).

The ADA

The FMLA is not the only law that entitles employees to take leave for health-related reasons. Granting leave to allow a disabled employee to seek treatment or recuperate can be an accommodation under the ADA. Unlike the FMLA, however, the ADA doesn't provide for a specific amount of leave. Instead, the employer must decide what is "reasonable" under the circumstances. How much leave is "reasonable" under the ADA depends on many factors, including the employee's position and the likelihood that he or she will be able to return in the foreseeable future. Don't assume that, once an employee's FMLA leave has been exhausted, the employer's ADA accommodation obligation has been satisfied. In some cases, more than 12 weeks of leave will be a reasonable accommodation.

Other ADA accommodations

In addition to time off from work, a disabled employee may be entitled to other reasonable accommodations in order to perform the essential functions of the job, including:

✓ Changing a work schedule.

✓ Providing adaptive devices (for example, a magnifying reader for a vision-impaired computer user).

✓ Modifying the job by removing non-essential functions.

✓ Reassigning the employee to a vacant position that better accommodates his or her disability.

✓ Making existing facilities accessible.

✓ Providing a reader or interpreter.

The employer is not required to remove essential job functions, or to lower quality or production standards, as an accommodation.

If an employee requests an accommodation, how should you respond?

✓ Discuss his or her needs with the employee, who is often in the best position to know what accommodation will be effective.

✓ If you were unaware of the disability or don't see a need for an accommodation, you may require the employee to provide documentation to support the accommodation request.

✓ You don't have to provide the precise accommodation the employee seeks if you can provide another effective accommodation.

Substance abuse

Most employers do not tolerate substance abuse in the workplace. Your employee handbook should state clear policies regarding drug and alcohol use. You can ban the use or possession of alcohol or illegal substances in your workplace, and forbid employees from coming to work impaired by drugs or alcohol. If your company is a government contractor or federal grant recipient, you may have additional obligations under the Drug Free Workplace Act.

The ADA also addresses substance abuse. Alcoholism is considered a disability for ADA purposes, along with rehabilitated drug abusers. Current drug addiction and casual drug use are not protected under the ADA. What does this mean for managers?

✓ Alcoholic employees are entitled to reasonable accommodation under the ADA, such as time off to seek treatment. Rehabilitated drug addicts are also entitled to reasonable accommodations.

✓ You can hold these employees to the same standards of performance and behavior as all other employees.

✓ You may not discriminate against alcoholics or rehabilitated drug abusers.

The ADA does not prohibit drug testing, but you should check your state laws to see if they impose any restrictions.

Minimum wage and overtime

Amended in 2007, the Fair Labor Standards Act (FLSA) will raise the minimum wage in stages to $7.25 in July 2009. The FLSA also governs overtime pay and requires that any employee who works more than 40 hours a week be paid at time and a half for those hours—unless the employee is "exempt." State laws may impose different minimum and overtime pay requirements by determining who is exempt, because the FLSA requirements centers on the nature of the employee's work and how he or she is paid. Generally speaking, non-supervisory employees who perform jobs requiring little independent thought or the exercise of discretion will not be deemed exempt. The job's title does not determine whether the employee is exempt or not. For example, though there is an exemption for "executives," an employee in the position of "executive assistant" who spends most of her day copying, filing, and typing will not be deemed exempt for FLSA purposes. In most cases, the employee must be salaried (not hourly), to qualify as exempt. The reverse is not true, however: Simply being paid a salary is not enough to make an employee exempt. The FLSA is one of the most complex employment laws, so always consult with employment counsel to ensure that your organization is in compliance.

Here are some common ways managers trip over the FLSA:

✓ Labeling an employee "exempt" in an effort to recognize the employee's contributions, when the employee doesn't qualify as exempt under the federal regulations.

✓ Assuming that everyone who is paid a salary is automatically exempt, regardless of their duties.

✓ Discouraging non-exempt employees from submitting claims for overtime pay.

✓ Giving non-exempt employees compensatory time in a subsequent workweek instead of overtime pay.

✓ Docking exempt employees' pay for absences of less than a full day (except for FMLA leave) if the employee has used up all his or her paid leave.

For more information, check the U.S. Department of Labor's Website (*www.dol.gov/esa/regs/compliance/whd/fairpay/main.htm*).

Termination

Despite your best efforts to hire and manage employees effectively, you may have to terminate someone's employment. Here are some key principles for minimizing your legal risk.

Be consistent

To avoid EEO and retaliation claims, that is, to stay within the law, make sure your termination decisions are consistent—and that similarly situated employees are disciplined to the same extent—or have a compelling, non-discriminatory business reason for singling out a particular employee differently.

Be fair

If the termination is due to continued poor performance, make sure you've given the employee clear notice of the problems and a reasonable chance to improve. Even if the employee doesn't appreciate your fair treatment, judges and juries do.

Follow procedure

Check your employee handbook and be sure to follow any termination procedures in it. Failure to do so could land you with a breach of contract claim or be used as evidence of discriminatory treatment in an EEO suit. If the employee has an employment agreement, make sure you've complied with its termination provisions.

Don't retaliate

If the employee has complained of an EEO violation or other employer misconduct, you could be accused of retaliation under the EEO or other employment statutes, or of wrongful discharge under state law. Make sure your termination decision is wholly unrelated to the employee's protected conduct, and be prepared to explain—and document—your legitimate business reason for the termination.

Consider requesting a signed release

A properly crafted release agreement, signed by the employee and accompanied by severance pay (or something else of value to which the employee wouldn't otherwise be entitled), will stop an employee from successfully pursuing a claim for damages.

Don't just recycle the release form you used in a previous termination. There are specific legal requirements for drafting enforceable releases, so always check with counsel when preparing a release agreement.

Pay final wages on time

Most state laws dictate when an employer must pay a departing employee his or her final paycheck, sometimes including accrued vacation pay. Those deadlines can be tight, so make sure you comply with the rules in your state.

Give neutral references, or be careful what you say

Providing substantive references entails some legal risk, particularly if the reference is negative or inaccurate, and costs the employee job opportunities elsewhere. Overly positive references also raise legal concerns. Consider following a "name, rank, and serial number" reference policy; that is, provide only dates of employment, last job title, and last salary.

If you prefer to share more information, here are some tips for minimizing risk:

- ✓ If one of your less-stellar employees requests a reference, politely suggest that he or she ask someone else. You have no obligation to provide a reference.
- ✓ If you do get asked for a reference, make sure the person seeking it really is a prospective employer. Ask for the name of the company and then call the person back using that company's main number.
- ✓ Ask about the nature of the position for which the employee is being considered, and limit your reference to discussing only attributes relevant to that position.
- ✓ Talk about only what you know is true, not what others have said or speculative observations.

Main message for managers

A host of employment law issues affects your management of human resources. You can't completely eliminate legal risk, but you can minimize the risk that an employee will sue you, or that an employee's lawsuit will be successful. Here are simple rules for doing so:

- ✓ Treat employees fairly and consistently, the way you would like to be treated.
- ✓ Follow your organization's published policies.
- ✓ Don't base employment decisions on stereotypes or assumptions, but on legitimate, non-discriminatory business reasons.
- ✓ If in doubt, check with an expert in your HR department or your employment counsel.

If you follow these rules, you'll not only minimize your legal risk, but also maximize the likelihood of making sound business decisions.

Author

Joyce Oliner has 20 years of experience practicing employment law and providing related training to managers, HR professionals, and line employees.

Chapter 10
Managing a Diverse Workforce

R-E-S-P-E-C-T...find out what it means to me.
—Aretha Franklin, Queen of Soul

The goal of a diversity strategy is an inclusive workplace—a work environment where everyone is welcomed and everyone is engaged in the work of the organization.

The changing workplace

In its 2004 survey and report "Preparing for the Workforce of Tomorrow," Hewitt Associates noted several nascent trends:

✓ Greater diversity in the labor pool. By 2008, women and minorities represent 70 percent of new entrants in the labor force, and by 2010, 34 percent of the U.S. workforce will be non-Caucasian.

✓ An aging workforce. By 2010, the 45–64 age group of the U.S. workforce will increase 29 percent, and the 65-plus group, will increase by 14 percent. The 18–44 age group, however, will see a 1-percent decline.

✓ By 2014, 75 percent of new workers will probably be from Asia; North America and Europe will contribute only 3 percent of the world's new labor force.

These trends tell us that focusing attention on managing a diverse workforce is not just a good idea—it is a business necessity. That attention used to be given to race and gender, but now we also look at diversity in age, ethnicity, physical ability or disability, sexual orientation, religion, and national origin and culture—and those are just the visible elements of diversity. We now need to address the invisible elements, such as diversity of thought, work experience, education, marital status, religious beliefs, socio-economic status, military experience, work style, communication style, and geography.

In today's complex, global environment, workplace diversity is really about creating a respectful, inclusive work environment where every employee has the opportunity to make a meaningful contribution to the organization's mission and goals.

How can diversity strategies tie into an organization's business objectives? Once the goal of enabling every employee to contribute is reached, the organization is able to:

✓ Attract and retain the best talent.

✓ Reduce the costs of high turnover, absenteeism, and low productivity.

✓ Have greater flexibility and adaptability in the rapidly changing marketplace.

✓ Increase sales and profits.

A Society for Human Resource Management (SHRM) study on how diversity affects the bottom line surveyed companies on

Fortune magazine's list of "Top 100 Companies to Work For." When the companies were asked how "diversity initiatives provide organizations with a competitive advantage by positive improvements in corporate culture, employee morale, retention, and recruitment":

✓ 40 percent said, "by ensuring leadership development programs reach all employees."

✓ 39 percent said, "by meeting the needs of diverse customers."

✓ 35 percent said, "by integrating diversity into the organization's business strategy."

✓ 34 percent said, "by increasing innovation by tapping employees of all backgrounds."

The Business Case for Diversity

Why the emphasis on diversity? Diversity is as much a business issue as it is a personal issue. Diversity provides a better return on the investment in human capital by helping to attract and retain the best, brightest, and most creative talent. As the marketplace and your customer base become more diverse, employing a diverse workforce allows you to capitalize on a diverse marketplace.

One of the biggest business drivers is the changing demographics. The ever-changing face of the U.S. population continues to reflect an increase in women, racial and ethnic groups, immigrants, older workers, and individuals with disabilities, as well as changing family structures and religious diversity.

While it is important to understand the demographics, it is equally important to move beyond representation issues and identify issues that create barriers to working effectively and productively with the marketplace. The challenge is to recognize that differences exist, respect those differences, and leverage them for the success of the organization.

—*Cornelia Gamlem*
President, The Gems Group, Herndon, Virginia

Establishing a diverse culture

Begin by being absolutely sure your organization's leadership supports, and will actively participate in, increasing employee diversity. Without that support, nothing else will succeed. The best way to get top leadership support for diversity is to make the case that a culture of diversity has a positive impact on the bottom line.

Once you have the support you need, review the organization's current policies, procedures, and practices to ensure they support diversity. If not, make any necessary changes, get the appropriate approvals, and announce the changes to employees.

Review the organization's Website to be sure its diversity-related material is true, useful, and meaningful. Potential clients and job candidates who visit the site want information that will help them determine whether they want to do business with or work for the organization.

Review the organization's intranet, if it has one, to be sure that the information available for employees states the commitment to diversity.

Use representative employee photos and stories on the Website and on the intranet that are natural and authentic. Include white men; women; people of various races, ethnicities, and generations; and people with a visible disability or other aspects of difference—but don't feel compelled to show all dimensions of diversity in every photo, which can detract from the impression of authenticity.

Review the strategic plan and the HR plan to be sure they support diversity. If they do not, work with the leadership to make the necessary changes.

Recruiting a diverse workforce

In the so-called knowledge economy, recruiting for diversity is an organizational strategy for business growth.

Top candidates seek organizations that have strong leadership and opportunities for growth. The tougher the labor market is for a particular job, the more effort is required to attract and hire minority candidates. Employers face increasing competition for the best talent—minority or not.

How can an organization position itself to find and keep the best?

One strategy for attracting diverse candidates is to update the organization's Website to ensure that the employment or career opportunity section includes the diversity policy and commitment. Bios and photos of diverse employees on the Website represent the opportunities for diversity in your organization. This can be a powerful recruiting tool. For other ideas, check the Websites of firms in your region that do a particularly good job of recruiting diverse candidates.

Some organizations rely heavily on certain sources for job candidates—and those sources may not yield a high number of minority applicants. Review recruiting sources your organization is using to be sure they will bring you the best talent. Look outside the traditional sources. (see "sources for minority applicants" at the end of this chapter.) If you rely heavily on employee referrals for new hires and your current workforce isn't diverse, you will not increase the diversity in your organization. Review the language in your organization's ads or online job postings to eliminate exclusionary words.

For example, besides recruiting at minority schools, investigate other universities that may have large minority populations. Use employees who personify your organization's current diversity to recruit at job fairs or on campus.

Once you've successfully recruited a minority candidate, the way you introduce him or her to your organization's culture (onboarding) is critical: If your organization has a mentoring program, get your diversity employees into it as early as possible. It is difficult enough for any new hire to merge into a new organization, but there are added challenges for minority employees.

Older workers

Although employers are rethinking their attitudes about older workers, several faulty perceptions persist:

✓ Older workers can't learn new skills. Yet people older than 50 are the fastest-growing group of Internet users.

✓ Older workers take more time off for illness than younger workers. In reality, attendance is higher among older workers.

✓ Older workers cost the organization more money to employ, but such costs as vacation and pensions are usually outweighed by the decrease in recruitment and training expenses because older workers tend to stay with an employer longer.

AARP has developed a National Employer Team in collaboration with companies that appreciate the talent older workers bring to the workplace. AARP serves as a clearinghouse for vetting the employers. Information on the National Employer Team and how firms can apply is available at *www.aarp.org/money/careers/findingajob/featuredemployers/info.html.*

"Allowing employees to ease into retirement or switch indefinitely to a more flexible schedule," says Diane Gold, president and founder of EEO Management Solutions, "can help maintain and facilitate the transfer of institutional knowledge. In a situation where employees are not given an option and want to reduce their schedule, they will often retire, finding alternative employment elsewhere."

It is to the employer's advantage to work with older employees and find ways to retain them, and their skills and knowledge.

Diversity committees and councils

Some employers establish groups that meet to foster and enhance diversity throughout the organization. Diversity committees sponsor activities such as celebrating Black History Month or holding potluck lunches where employees are encouraged to bring a dish from their culture. Diversity councils, in contrast, require top management support to have an impact on the organization. All employees should be encouraged to participate on the council or committee.

When selecting people to serve on a diversity council, consider including those who:

✓ Have differing viewpoints, so that employees feel their views are being represented on the council.

✓ Are adaptable and flexible.

✓ Are respected in the organization, so the council's recommendations are credible.

✓ Can manage their own biases and be open to listening to others.

✓ Are passionate about diversity.

✓ Have specific skills the council needs at times.

✓ Can view the organization as a whole and see diversity as part of its strategic goals.

Some diversity councils assume certain responsibilities, which can include:

✓ Communicating information on affirmative action, cultural diversity, and equal opportunity employment to all employees.

✓ Developing diversity policies and guidelines for the workforce.

✓ Educating the workforce about issues involving diversity and inclusion.

✓ Bringing new diversity-related information to management.

✓ Relaying employees' concerns regarding diversity issues to management.

Measuring the impact of diversity

How will you know when you have achieved a diverse and inclusive workplace?

✓ There is a wide range of communication and thinking styles, and everyone is encouraged to share new ideas.

✓ The organization casts "wide net" to attract diverse job applicants.

✓ The working environment is friendly and welcoming to everyone, including new employees.

✓ Employees from different cultures share ideas and resources.

✓ Diversity is visible at all levels of the organization.

✓ All organizational materials—including the Website, marketing information, and recruitment materials— reflect your workplace's various genders, races, sexual orientations, religions, physical abilities, national origins, ages, and any other dimensions of diversity represented among employees.

Main message for managers

Successful managers know that a diverse and fully engaged workforce gives their organization a competitive advantage. Managers must actively seek out diverse employees, carefully introduce them into the organization, and use the diversity of thought and experience they bring to maximum effectiveness.

Sources for minority applicants

African-American Career World magazine
www.eop.com/aacw.html

American Jewish World Service
www.ajws.org/index.cfm

The Black Collegian
http://black-collegian.com

Black Enterprise
http://blackenterprise.com

National Black MBA Association
www.nbmba.org

Black MBA Magazine
www.blackmbamagazine.net

National Hispanic Business Association
www.nhba.org

Hispanic Career World
http://eop.com

Careers & the DISabled
http://eop.com

LATPRO Hispanic Jobs
www.latpro.com

Project Hired
http://kings.projecthired.org/public

HireDiversity.com
www.hirediversity.com

Indian Country Today
http://indiancountry.com

Native American Employment Opportunities
http://hanksville.org/NAresources/indices/NAjobs.html

Veterans Enterprise
www.veteransenterprise.com

Veterans' Vision
www.vetsvision.org/vetsvision.html

Women's Business Enterprise National Council
www.wbenc.org

HispanicOnline
www.hispaniconline.com

AfricanAmericanJobsite.com
www.africanamericanjobsite.com

DiversityLink.com
www.diversitylink.com

Diversity Search
www.diversitysearch.com

iHispano.com
http://ihispano.com

Saludos.com
http://saludos.com

Workforce50
Workforce50.com

Quintessential Careers
http://quintcareers.com/mature_jobseekers.html

Chapter 11
Technology

We shape our tools and then our tools shape us.
—Marshall McLuhan, visionary "guru" of media culture

S taying current with technology can give your company an important competitive advantage that put you above the other companies.

Change is a constant

We live in a world where face-to-face communication has just about disappeared. Rather than go to a travel agent to book a trip, we book travel ourselves, online. We do our banking online or via voice-activated phone systems.

Technology has changed most of our business practices. But when dealing with "people issues," nothing can replace a face-to-face conversation. Managers must know when and how to use technology.

Only a short time ago, business was conducted by either phone or letter. Now we use e-mail, voice mail, and instant messaging to communicate immediately with business colleagues. We often meet by conference call or on the Web, and it is not unusual for people who work near each other to communicate online.

These new tools are making employers create new policies concerning privacy. And what about blogs? Some organizations encourage employees to blog, and others prohibit it. With the advent of PDAs (personal digital assistants, such as Palm or BlackBerry handhelds), it's possible for employees to be connected with work 24 hours a day, seven days a week!

Technology has also had a major impact on organizations' management of people issues throughout the past 15 years. Today, many formerly labor-intensive, time-consuming tasks have been automated. However, savvy managers know when to leave voice mail and e-mail behind and sit down with an employee for a conversation.

Although using technology to manage processes is no longer just an option, organizations must be careful to ensure that any use of technology tools jibes with their strategic goals (see Chapter 1).

The use of technology also reflects generational differences: Many employees in the Veteran and Baby Boomer generations (ages 55-plus) prefer face-to-face meetings and conversations, whereas the younger generations are typically more comfortable with technology. Managers should consider their employees' comfort level with technology in deciding how best to communicate with them. Some people prefer e-mail; others would rather use the phone or meet in person. When there is information to be shared that everyone needs to hear, it certainly makes sense to send an e-mail.

This chapter explores how managers can use technology to manage the people parts of their jobs.

Sample technology policies

Organizations' employee handbooks should include policies on the use of phones, e-mail, IM, and personal electronic devices. If your organization doesn't have such a handbook, we recommend requiring employees to sign an acknowledgment of the organization's policy on electronic devices and material. It is important to include in all these policies a statement such as:

"All communications that are sent or received from [name of organization]'s computers are its sole property and may be monitored. Employees are required, upon request, to share passwords with their supervisors or authorized IT staff but are not permitted to share passwords with other employees."

Sample e-mail policy

E-mail is intended primarily for business communication among coworkers, suppliers, and customers. Incidental personal use of [organization name]'s e-mail system is permitted, as long as it is on the employee's own time and does not interfere with his or her job responsibilities or [organization]'s business operation.

Without notice and at any time, [organization] may read all e-mails, personal address books, and other information stored on its computers. Employees' use of [organization]'s e-mail system constitutes acceptance of the internal monitoring policy.

Employees should use good judgment when composing e-mail and should assume that their messages will be reviewed and retained by someone other than the recipient.

Prohibited uses of e-mail include any illegal activity, pornography, gambling, or statements of violence, racism, or harassment. Misuse of the e-mail system may result in disciplinary action, up to and including termination of employment.

Sample phone policy

While [organization] understands that employees occasionally need to make or receive personal phone calls during work hours, please limit personal calls to emergencies only. Employees will reimburse [organization] for personal toll or long-distance calls made on its phones. Use of personal cell phones is limited to break time. Excessive personal phone usage may result in disciplinary action, up to and including termination.

Sample instant messaging policy

Employees are expected to limit their use of instant messages (IM) to work-related subjects. Instant messaging should not be used to transmit confidential, proprietary, or personal employee information. It is most appropriate for sending brief information such as a phone number, address, purchase order, or similar data. Instant messaging is never a substitute for a face-to-face conversation with coworkers or other work-related people. Employees are prohibited from using personal encryption software for instant messages sent via the organization's equipment.

All instant messages are captured by [organization]'s system software and are subject to management review. [Organization] reserves the right to disclose the content of instant messages or other electronic communication to third parties, without notice to the employee.

Improper use of instant messaging may result in disciplinary action, up to and including termination of employment. Examples of improper instant messages or e-mails include:

- ✓ Inappropriate messages such as those including racial, religious, ethnic, or sexual slurs.
- ✓ Foul language.
- ✓ Illegal or harassing messages.
- ✓ Chain messages or sports pools.
- ✓ Any use that violates [organization] policy.

Sample personal electronic devices policy

Employees should limit their use of personal electronic devices to areas where that use does not disturb others. When using personal electronic devices, employees must not put themselves or others at risk.

Sample blogging policy

Personal Websites and blogs (originally called Web logs) are common methods of self-expression in our culture. [Organization] respects the rights of employees who wish to use these media during personal time. However, the following requirements apply to any employee who identifies him- or herself as an employee of [organization] on a Website or blog:

- ✓ It must be stated that the views expressed are those of the individual and not necessarily the views of [organization].
- ✓ No confidential or proprietary information about [organization] or any of its clients or customers can be disclosed.
- ✓ No defamatory statements may be made about the organization or its employees, clients, customers, or competitors.
- ✓ Blogging and personal Websites must not interfere with work commitments.

If a blog is determined to be harmful to the firm, the employee may be requested to stop the activity or face possible disciplinary action.

Managing HR information and processes

Today's managers have to think and operate differently from their predecessors to keep up with innovations in business. One of the challenges in managing people is keeping track of all the information the organization needs to retain and manage employees. Technology offers a solution: software collectively called Human Resources Information System (HRIS).

HRIS can be used for, among other tasks, planning and tracking:

✓ Benefits, such as insurance and retirement plans.

✓ Payroll administration and processing.

✓ Salary administration.

✓ Employee data; personnel and organizational changes.

✓ Recruiting and orientation.

✓ Work hours, attendance, time off, and labor cost distribution.

✓ Disciplinary actions.

✓ Performance appraisals.

✓ High-potential employees (for succession candidates).

✓ Training attendance and skills inventories.

If your organization does not use HRIS yet, the following suggestions will help you select a vendor and implement a system.

Selecting an HRIS program is complex and time-consuming, but it's time well spent given the long-term implications for the organization. Begin by looking at the aspects of your business that drive your organization to implement a new system, and determine how an HRIS will support your overall requirements. This may involve meeting with senior leaders and others to identify what they need from HR.

Next, determine the specifics of those requirements: Are you looking for a system that includes job-applicant tracking, or are you more focused on training records, or the administration of government-mandated programs such as HIPAA or COBRA? Will your employees be comfortable with self-service applications—accessing information online about benefits, for example, rather than calling or visiting HR staff? An employer's desire to reduce costs, however, may outweigh the employees' preferences for more personal attention.

What about future requirements? What are your growth projections? Are you planning to implement an online system for job applicants?

When planning and choosing an HRIS, involving the organization's IT department is crucial: Should you use a standalone PC, networked client/server, or mainframe system? What operating system will it run—Windows, MacIntosh (Apple), Unix, or something else? Will the HRIS be used in multiple locations? Does the organization already have computer and software systems with which the HRIS will interface?

Once those questions are answered, document the requirements as specifically as possible so you can choose the right vendor. If it's difficult to clarify goals and requirements at this point, now may not be the right time to move forward. Wait until those are clear so as not to waste time and other resources.

Before seeking vendors, determine how much the organization is willing to spend on software, hardware, and implementation—and develop a budget. This might be hard to do before even talking with vendors, but you should have at least a "ballpark" figure in mind. Software costs include licensing fees, database licenses, and maintenance. Hardware includes servers, PCs, laptops, and network upgrades. Implementation costs include training, consulting services from the vendor, and data entry.

One final step before approaching vendors: Determine whether your IT department has the ability and capacity to build a system that will meet the requirements. Having IT build your system can seem an attractive method for getting what you need, it is time-consuming: How quickly can the work be accomplished?

The best way to find vendors is to network with others in your field and ask what systems they use. The Society for Human

Resource Management (SHRM) has buyers' guides on its Website, which is a good place to start finding potential vendors. Once you have identified some, request product information.

The next step is to prepare a request for proposal (RFP) or a simpler request for information (RFI). It should provide information about your organization and a link to your Website, your requirements for an HRIS, and technical specifications, as well as ask for pricing and references. Finally, your request should seek information on customer support and training, and a sample of the vendor's contract terms.

A Paperless HR Department

"Consider what Arte Nathan was able to do as VP for HR for the Bellagio Hotel. Confronted with the challenge of completely staffing when it first opened in 1998, he turned to technology. He developed an entirely paperless application process, capturing 75,000 applications in less than five months, hiring almost 10,000 people. This data then became the foundation for providing managers with electronic access to personnel files. Reliance on technology allowed HR to focus on the strategy of picking the right people—employees who would provide great customer service—which in turn helped make the Bellagio one of the top hotels in Las Vegas."[1]

When you receive the vendors' responses to the RFP or RFI, create a spreadsheet so you can easily compare them and decide which three or four vendors to invite for a product demonstration. In your invitation, specify what software products you want the vendors to show you.

Before each demonstration, assemble a list of questions to ask the vendor. Be sure that everyone involved in the decision can attend the demos, including the IT staff, whose questions for the vendors will be different from those asked by managers or HR staff.

After a demonstration, ask all attending staff members for their opinions, so that you can list the positives and negatives of each product. Check the finalists' references and, if possible, visit one of the references' workplaces to see the product in action. Meet with each finalist to review once more the programs' features, costs, customer service, product support, and implementation plans.

Before making the final decision, sift through all the information you have gathered. If the requirements have been set, the vendors carefully evaluated, and the references checked, the right decision should be clear. If the choice is not obvious, go back to the finalists for additional information or to negotiate better terms.

Applicant tracking

If the HRIS you chose does not have an applicant-tracking function, or if the organization isn't ready for an HRIS but does need a way to track job openings and candidates, there are stand-alone systems for applicant tracking that store résumés and, via keyword search, let you retrieve those that match current openings. Most systems also track a candidate's progress through various stages of recruitment—screenings by phone, interviews, rejections, and offers.

Selecting a vendor for an applicant-tracking system works the same way as selecting an HRIS vendor. Among the features you may require are:

✓ Candidate tracking.
✓ Job requisition management.
✓ Résumé management.

✓ Interview scheduling.

✓ Communications with candidates, such as letters of rejection or offers.

✓ Meeting external reporting requirements, such as for EEO laws or government-contract compliance.

✓ Internal reporting requirements (the time it takes to fill positions, the cost per hire or requisitions per recruiter, and so forth).

Vendor Selection Criteria

When you evaluate potential vendors for HRIS or applicant-tracking systems, Kerri Koss Morehart, HR director for Pragmatics, Inc., suggests asking:

✓ *What is the vendor's customer-service philosophy? How long does it take to respond to its customers?*

✓ *Can you access the vendor's customer service by e-mail, phone, or Internet?*

✓ *How often does the vendor upgrade its system?*

✓ *How long has the vendor been in business?*

✓ *How many customers does it have currently, and what is its client-retention rate?*

✓ *Is the system easy to learn so that new staff members can pick it up quickly?*

✓ *Does the vendor provide on-site training and support?*

E-learning

Electronic learning, or e-learning, is widely used in academia for online classes—an advantage for working-adult students in particular. As the technology for learning by computer improved in the 1980s, many organizations added computer-based training (CBT) to their resources. The latest technologies have driven e-learning well beyond CBT.

E-learning works especially well for organizations that are geo-graphically dispersed, but it can also be used in combination with face-to-face training (known as blended learning). It is highly cost-effective, as the materials can be used multiple times, but the tech-nology to create e-learning can be expensive up front. E-learning media include Webcasts, vcasts (video), podcasts, and multi-media CD-ROMs and DVDs. The material can be used not only on com-puters but also on PDAs and MP3 players.

Note that Webcasts, particularly, are also often used for com-munication with internal staff in regional offices, saving the costs of travel to the "home office" for meetings.

Main message for managers

Technology has a major effect on everything we do as manag-ers. It is up to us whether that effect is positive or negative. New technologies have created some managerial challenges, including how information is shared within and outside the organization on Websites and in e-mails, instant messages, and blogs.

Using technology to manage tasks such as payroll, benefits administration, time and attendance, and personnel files frees HR staff and managers to focus on more strategic actions that have the most impact on the organization. The new realities of the work-place demand that we all learn about and adjust to new technolo-gies, now and into the future.

Chapter 12
21st-Century
Workplace Challenges

Progress might have been all right once, but it has gone on too long.
—Ogden Nash

The modern workplace is evolutionary, with resources—human and otherwise—in a state of constant flux. How organizations adapt and react can mean the difference between success and failure.

Workforce changes

The workplace has changed significantly in this new century, and the pace of change isn't slowing down. We have moved into a global economy in which events and actions in formerly remote parts of the world have a real impact on U.S. business. We've moved into the knowledge economy, too: The service industry has replaced manufacturing as the core U.S. enterprise.

Work that used to be done here is being "outsourced" to countries that pay lower wages. Technology is changing how and where we work. Employees are seeking a balance between their work and personal lives.

Meanwhile, the makeup of the labor pool in this country continues to experience major shifts. The U.S. Department of Labor estimates that by 2008, 70 percent of people entering the job market will be women and minorities. Further, we may face a significant labor shortage—depending on whether Baby Boomers (those born 1946–1964) retire when they are eligible or continue to work at least part-time.[1]

These forecasts suggest that organizations should review their current policies and practices to be sure they are prepared for a different workforce.

Business ethics

Recent scandals have raised the bar considerably regarding workplace ethics—that is, moral principles and values that establish appropriate conduct. More than half of U.S. businesses report having some type of ethics policy—but that isn't enough. For example, Enron Corporation, a fast-growing energy firm that was brought down by accounting scandals in the early 21st century, had a comprehensive ethics policy that appears to have been ignored. In addition to the Enron scandal, firms such as WorldCom, Tyco International, and Arthur Anderson (auditors to both Enron and WorldCom) were greatly affected by their leaders' unethical actions.

What can we do to be sure our organizations follow ethical practices? Many organizations are asking their HR departments to serve as the "conscience of the organization" and monitor behavior. Policies aren't enough; employees need to see others, at all levels of the organization, conduct themselves ethically. Managers need to ensure that their organizational cultures demand ethical behavior. Organization leaders should participate in determining what their ethics codes cover, then hold each manager accountable for ensuring that those standards are met. Most important, managers must be models of ethical behavior at all times.

Ethical issues for top management to grapple with include, but are not limited to:

✓ What information should be shared with employees?

✓ How much information should the employer share regarding a former employee who was fired or laid off?

✓ What impact should an employee's personal life have on his or her potential for advancement?

✓ Should the organization make accommodations for a valued employee whose job performance is suffering because of a personal situation?

✓ Should employees be responsible for reporting actions they think violate the organization's ethics? If so, to what extent or under what procedure?

Suggestions for codifying ethical behavior in an organization include having a written statement that is published and posted around your workplace, then following that code of ethics; discussing your code of ethics in the orientation process and then conducting mandatory, annual ethics training for everyone; informing employees on how to report an ethics violation and ensuring that those who report them are not subject to retaliation; setting up a confidential hotline for reporting ethics violations; and encouraging continuing discussion of ethics in staff meetings.

Code of Ethics

Among the elements of workplace issues and behavior that a code of ethics might cover are:

✓ *Applicable laws.*

✓ *Confidential or proprietary material.*

✓ *Conflicts of interest.*

✓ *Organizational assets or property.*

✓ *Acceptance of gifts, gratuities, and entertainment.*

✓ *Privacy issues.*

✓ *Dealing with the media.*

✓ *Reporting ethics violations, including a non-retaliation statement.*

Since the recent spate of ethics scandals, Congress passed the Sarbanes-Oxley Act of 2002 (SOX), which is having a large impact on the policies and procedures for publicly held companies.

Sarbanes-Oxley Act of 2002

The Sarbanes-Oxley Act of 2002, commonly referred to as SOX, is also known as the Public Company Accounting Reform and Investor Act of 2002, a federal law enacted in response to a spate of major corporate and accounting scandals that diminished public trust in accounting practices.

SOX established new or enhanced standards for the governing boards of all U.S. public companies, management, and public accounting firms. It also established the Public Company Accounting Oversight Board, charged with overseeing, regulating, inspecting, and disciplining accounting firms in their roles as auditors of public companies. SOX also covers issues such as auditor independence, corporate governance, internal control assessment, and enhanced financial disclosure.

The law significantly expanded protection for employees who allege certain types of corporate misconduct. SOX allows the following employees to bring a lawsuit for reinstatement, back pay, and damages if they have been retaliated against for reporting corporate fraud or accounting abuses: employees of publicly traded companies and employees of any entity, public or private, that is a contractor to a publicly traded company such as an accounting firm. SOX also imposes criminal penalties—including up to 10 years imprisonment—on anyone who retaliates against a person for providing true information to a law enforcement officer about the commission of a federal crime.

For additional information on the Sarbanes-Oxley Act of 2002, contact your organization's employment-law counsel.

Generations at work

For the first time in history, four generations are at work, which presents some interesting challenges. Americans are living and working longer. Those demographic changes in the workforce and the increasing desire for more flexible hours will mean that more than just large employers will offer flexibility. As the population ages, more and more workers will need to care for aging parents, while younger workers will still need to care for children.

A survey by AARP/Roper Starch Worldwide Inc., found that almost 80 percent of Baby Boomers plan to work at least part-time after retirement.[2]

This trend affects organizations on several levels:

✓ Boomers aren't retiring, which blocks promotions for younger workers.

✓ Employers with older workers may experience higher healthcare costs.

✓ Leave policies (sick and vacation) may need revamping to provide more flexibility in situations where the Family and Medical Leave Act doesn't apply.

The generation about which the senior-management Boomers know the least is the Millennial Generation, or Generation Y.

As Generation X and Millennials take control of organizations, work/life balance and workplace flexibility may rival health insurance and retirement benefits to become the top concerns of employees, and the American workplace will be changed forever.

It will also be a challenge as Generation X employees (those born 1965–1977) take on increasingly significant managerial roles in organizations and supervise Baby Boomers and Veterans (born before 1946).

The Millennial Generation is coming right behind Generation X, and these employees are more optimistic and entrepreneurial than previous generations. This generation's sense of entitlement will be a challenge for managers. Millennials (those born 1978–1990) want to be entertained, and they are creative, innovative, and resourceful. They don't understand what the world was like before laptops, e-mail, and text messaging.

Although there are differences among the generations, all of us want the same things at work:

✓ Respect.

✓ Fair treatment.

✓ Equality.

✓ Balance.

✓ Flexibility.

✓ Feedback.

✓ Job enhancement and advancement opportunities.[3]

Let's look at each of the four generations at work.

Veterans (born before 1946)

They expected to build a career with one employer or perhaps in a single field with a small number of employers. Smart organizations are asking Veterans to stay or return to work as trainers or recruiters, where they are able to share their experiences and leave a legacy.

Some positives of the Veteran Generation:

✓ Dependable.

✓ Detail-oriented.

✓ Thorough.

✓ Loyal.

✓ Hardworking.

Some challenges they face:

✓ Don't like ambiguity or change.

✓ Reluctant to "make waves."

✓ Averse to conflict.

✓ Don't like to discuss feelings.

Baby Boomers (1946–1964)

They have always wanted to excel in their careers, and many have already reached the point of considering what to do with the rest of their lives. Smart organizations are looking for projects that will engage Boomers so their intellectual capital doesn't walk out the door.

Some positives of the Baby Boom Generation:

✓ Optimistic.

✓ Driven.

✓ Go the extra mile.

✓ Team players.

✓ Want to please others.

✓ Good at building relationships.

Some challenges they face:

✓ Self-centered.

✓ Judgmental.

✓ Averse to conflict.

Generation X (1965–1977)

They are the dominant force in today's business environment. Their approach to work is fundamentally different from that of their seniors because many in this generation were "latchkey kids" and learned self-reliance at an early age. Therefore, they will not tolerate being micromanaged, and they need to give and receive frequent feedback. They saw their parents go through downsizings and lay-offs, so they don't put much trust in organizational loyalty or job security.

Some positives of Generation X:

✓ Adaptable.

✓ Tech-savvy.

✓ Self-reliant.

✓ Not intimidated by authority.

✓ Creative.

✓ Informal.

✓ Pragmatic.

Some challenges they face:

✓ Impatient.

✓ Lack people skills.

✓ Cynical.

✓ Consider work "just a job."

Millennials (1978–1990)
(aka Generation Y or Generation Why)

They have heard from an early age that they need to build portfolios to get into the right college to land the right job. They are used to doing many things at once and are so technologically savvy that their family and friends use them as tech support; Millennials must be "connected" at all times. They will probably have several careers in very different fields, so retaining this generation will be a challenge for employers, but, if their organizations offer development opportunities, they may stay a little longer. This generation is the most socially conscious of any since the 1960s.

Some positives of the Millennial Generation:

✓ Like structure.

✓ Optimistic.

✓ Self-confident.

✓ Goal-oriented.

✓ Inclusive.

✓ Multi-taskers.

✓ Tech-savvy.

Some challenges they face:

✓ Need structure.

✓ Inexperienced.

✓ Need constant feedback.

✓ Entitlement mentality.

Four Generations

Veterans

Born 1922–1945

Influenced by:

✓ *Charles Lindbergh's 1927 flight across the Atlantic Ocean.*

✓ *Stock market crash of 1929.*

✓ *Social Security established in 1934.*

✓ *World War II.*

✓ *Hiroshima.*

Baby Boomers

Born 1946–1964

Influenced by:

✓ *Civil Rights movement.*

✓ *Space exploration.*

✓ *Vietnam War.*

✓ *Assassinations of John and Bobby Kennedy and Martin Luther King Jr.*

Generation X

Born 1965–1977
Influenced by:
✓ *Watergate.*
✓ *Introduction of the personal computer in 1981.*
✓ *Stock market crash of 1987.*
✓ *Gulf War.*

Millennial Generation

Born 1978–1990
Influenced by:
✓ *Oklahoma City bombing in 1995.*
✓ *Columbine massacre in 1999.*
✓ *September 11th attacks in 2001.*
✓ *E-mail and instant messaging.*

Work/life balance

Most people in the workforce want a full and balanced life, but it is only in recent years that they have raised their voices about it.

Janet Luhrs, a Seattle-based attorney, left that highly paid field to have a better work/life balance. The author of *The Simple Life Guide*,[4] she started *Simple Living* magazine in 1992 and began winning attention for her ideas on "voluntary simplicity." She and others struck a chord with many Americans who longed to spend less time on the job and more time with family and friends. After the attacks of September 11, 2001, many stories in the press noted that executives were walking away from careers they had spent a lifetime building.

Few people can actually take that step, so they look to their employers for the flexibility to keep their positions, yet have time for activities outside the office.

Responding to employees' need for an alternative work schedule enhances the organization's ability to compete in the 21st century.

Employers, too, are looking for greater flexibility—to compete in the global economy. That has created a trend toward alternative staffing arrangements, including hiring independent contractors rather than full-time employees, or maintaining an "on-call" workforce for peak periods. These types of arrangements help employers avoid a cycle of hires and layoffs as they respond to market forces.

Employees are already beginning to see themselves as "free agents" whose skills matter more than where they work. Many now present themselves as being available for work on a project-by-project basis, and many organizations bring laid-off employees back as independent contractors. This decreases organizations' fixed-salary and benefits costs while the work still gets done.

To implement alternative staffing, employers must first determine which functions are "core" to the business (for example, those that bring in revenue) and work hard to retain the employees who perform them, then design a structure that accommodates the use of independent contractors, part-timers, or seasonal workers for other positions.

Another approach employers can use is to institute flextime, establishing core business hours when all employees must be present. Employees work with their managers to determine their own work hours. This allows for such needs as childcare and medical appointments. This avoids the problem of employees having to ask for time off—or being late or leaving early—and their managers know when to expect them on the job.

Daycare and doctor visits aren't the only reasons employees want flexibility. Older workers may want to ease into retirement, adult children may need time to care for elderly parents, and other employees might want to train for an athletic event or volunteer for a favorite charity. Today's fathers often want the same work/life balance and scheduling options as working mothers, yet may fear being stigmatized if and when they use flex benefits.

The generation currently entering the workforce is more likely than older ones to request and expect alternative work arrangements, whether it is telecommuting from home one day a week or working a compressed week. This new generation of workers calls for a new view of how work is measured, especially when "face time" is no longer an adequate way to judge whether an employee is doing a good job.

At DuPont, employees who took advantage of work/life and flexibility programs were more committed to their jobs and less "burned out,"[5] a 2002 report found. The First Tennessee Bank found through research that its most profitable branches were those with the happiest employees. The bank asked employees what was required for them to be happy at work, and the answer was flexibility. Throughout a three-year period, the bank's customer-retention rate increased to 95 percent (compared to the industry standard of 88 percent).[6]

All these strategies can have a positive impact on employees and the level of their engagement at work. Each organization should determine what is important to its workforce and then, and only then, design plans to address issues of work/life balance, telework, and flextime. One size does *not* fit all.

Telework

Telework is a very different way of doing business, with its own positive and negative aspects. "Work is what you do—not where you go," says John Edwards of Telework Consortiums, based in Leesburg, Virginia.

Innovative technologies enable employees to work from off-site locations. In most cases, that location is in their homes, but some cities are setting up so-called Telework Centers in remote parts of their metropolitan areas, giving employees shorter commutes to places fully equipped with state-of-the-art technology.

Telework moves the work to the worker electronically; telecommuting is a type of teleworking in which an employee travels to his or her employer's office less often than before.

Pros and Cons of Telework for Organizations

Pros

✓ **Lower real estate investment.** *Organizations may be able to decrease their office space. Some allocate the same space to several employees, who use it at different times. Although coordination is needed to ensure adequate work space for each day, this is extremely cost-effective.*

✓ **Increased productivity.** *Employees working from home typically have fewer distractions (such as drop-in visits from coworkers) than those working onsite. Productivity can also increase as employees spend less time commuting, allowing more time to work.*

✓ **Reduced sick leave costs.** *When employees can work from home, they don't use sick days as often as when they must go to the work site.*

✓ **Reduced healthcare costs.** *If employees can work from home with a minor illness, healthcare costs may decrease because fewer colds and viruses will spread through the office.*

✓ **Increased the labor pool.** *Making employers attractive to semi-retired workers, homemakers, and people who cannot commute brings in new talent and helps retain highly valued employees.*

✓ **Expanded customer service.** *Employees can serve customers after normal business hours or when the central office is closed for emergencies such as inclement weather and natural disasters.*

Cons

✓ *Some managers find it difficult to manage employees they can't see, and therefore may be less likely to promote deserving teleworkers.*

✓ *The cost of technology to support telework can be high.*

✓ *Because some positions don't lend themselves to teleworking, morale problems can surface between employees who can and those who cannot.*

An organization that decides to implement a telework program should first:

✓ *Obtain senior management support.*

✓ *Determine what new technology resources will be required.*

✓ *Develop guidelines for the program.*

✓ *Determine which positions (not people!) will be eligible.*

✓ *Develop a strategy to announce the program to all employees.*

✓ *Train managers and teleworkers.*

Outsourcing

Outsourcing human resources is gaining popularity with companies that can't afford or don't want to hire an extra person or a team for particular functions such as payroll or benefits administration.

The most frequently outsourced HR functions are[7]:

✓ 401(k) administration.

✓ Pre-employment testing/assessment.

✓ Background checking.

✓ Flexible spending account administration.

✓ Employee assistance programs.

✓ Health care benefits and COBRA administration.

✓ Temporary staffing.

✓ Pension benefits administration.

✓ Retirement benefits administration.

✓ Relocation.

✓ Payroll.

✓ Retirement planning.

Advantages

✓ **HR staff can be more strategic.** If routine tasks are outsourced, HR can focus on tasks that have more impact on the organization's bottom line.

✓ **Compliance issues.** Vendors that specialize in the legal aspects of HR matters can provide the information required for the company to comply with applicable laws.

✓ **Efficiency.** If the outsourcing firm specializes in a particular area, it should be able to do as much work as company staff, in less time.

Disadvantages

✓ **Employer privacy.** Some organizations don't want outside vendors to know significant aspects of their business.

✓ **Employee reaction.** Current employees may feel less connected to the organization if personal issues such as benefits or salaries are outsourced.

✓ **Employee relations.** Companies that provide outsourcing may not handle such issues as sensitively as on-staff HR professionals. This could create issues that require the organization to step in and handle sticky situations.

Outsourcing Checklist for Employers

In deciding whether to outsource, an organization should consider the following questions:

✓ *What do we spend on the tasks we may want to outsource?*

✓ *How would outsourcing affect our current workforce, especially if it entails eliminating positions?*

✓ *Who will coordinate with the outsourcing firm, and how will doing so affect that employee's workload?*

✓ *What criteria should we use in choosing an outsourcing firm? For example, do we want to hire a firm that would keep outsourced functions in this country, or one that could or would send the functions offshore?*

Globalization

Customers are all over the world, thanks to the Internet. So are many employees. Some organizations have offices around the world, and others are owned by foreign investors.

Today's managers need to stay up-to-date on world events and the global economy to work with customers and employees in other countries, and evaluate whether such events will affect their organization's business or employee base. They need training in managing across frontiers.

Employees on foreign assignment should be trained in cross-cultural communication, cultural adaptability, and the language of the assigned country.

Wellness programs

With healthcare costs skyrocketing, the single most effective strategy for cost containment is to promote a healthy lifestyle through behavioral change.

Smoking is the leading cause of preventable death in the United States. According to the Centers for Disease Control, about 30 percent of adults smoke cigarettes, and approximately 438,000 deaths a year are associated with smoking. The second leading cause is obesity, which increases the risk of developing at least 30 serious medical conditions, and is associated with increases in deaths from all causes, according to the American Obesity Association.

Aon Consulting, a multinational risk-management consulting firm, reports that:

- ✓ 67 percent of Americans are overweight compared to Europeans.
- ✓ 60 percent of Americans don't engage in enough physical activity.
- ✓ 6 to 14 percent of U.S. medical costs are attributed to smoking.
- ✓ About 50 percent of U.S. adults eat fast food every day.
- ✓ 70 percent of all deaths are due to chronic disease.
- ✓ Chronic disease accounts for 75 percent of U.S. healthcare costs.

Managers should consider supporting a wellness program in their organizations that encourages employees to adopt a healthier lifestyle. That should not only improve the employees' health, but also boost the bottom line.

Tips for a Successful Wellness Program

✓ *Involve employees' family members in your wellness program.*

✓ *Sponsor health screenings at the workplace.*

✓ *Provide incentives for employees to stop smoking.*

✓ *Encourage participation in the program with incentives, after finding out which ones might work with your employees.*

✓ *Consider weight-loss programs such as Weight Watchers at Work.*

✓ *If there is no health club at the office, subsidize membership at a local club through payroll deduction.*

✓ *Reduce stress by offering chair massages at a discount one day a week.*

"Across the country," says Cheryl Mirabella, an HR trainer and the founder of Living Whole Health, "companies are beginning to take notice of the startling connections between employee wellness and fiscal responsibility, and look for better answers. Employee wellness programs not only boost morale, but make significant, measurable differences in healthcare spending. Studies have shown that *employee wellness programs help companies reduce their healthcare costs an average of $3.72* for each dollar invested." (*Emphasis added.*)

Main message for managers

Managing people in the 21st century seems to entail new challenges at every turn. Managers need to be aware of current events to stay ahead of new trends and issues. To take their organizations forward to the future, they should:

✓ Prepare for an increasing number of women and minorities in the workforce.

✓ Develop a code of ethics and monitor compliance with it.

✓ Maximize the positive aspects so as to minimize the differences among generations in the workforce.

✓ Create opportunities for employees to have work/life balance and flexibility.

✓ Carefully evaluate whether outsourcing will benefit the organization.

✓ Provide training on cross-cultural issues for both managers and employees.

Afterword

Here's a final, important thought on being a good manager and/or HR professional. Never forget that your most important resource is your employees. Do all you can to create an environment that motivates and engages them.

A study conducted by the Labor Relations Institute of New York in 1946 found that the two motivators most valued by white-collar, non-supervisory employees were "full appreciation for work done," closely followed by "feeling 'in on things.'" When the study was repeated in 1981 and again in 1994, those values were topped by "interesting work." In all three years, employees ranked "good wages" only fifth among 10 motivating factors. But when immediate *supervisors* were asked what motivated their employees, in all three years they ranked good wages first, job security second, and promotion/growth third.[1]

In the book *The Enthusiastic Employee: How Companies Profit by Giving Workers What They Want*, the authors—David Sirota, Louis Mischkind, and Michael Irwin Meltzer—reported the results of more than 30 years of survey research covering millions of workers at all leves and all industries.[2] Conducted at Sirota Survey Intelligence, this research "reveals enduring and near-universal truths about workers and shows which of the prevailing views of executives are no more than myths," according to a white paper based on the book.

The paper acknowledges that:

[N]o two individuals are precisely alike, and these differences need to be taken [into] account in the management of people. But it is also true that there are broad and useful generalizations—grounded in empirical research—that can be made about people at work. For example, it is clear that, while there are differences in degree, the overwhelming majority of people do want to be proud of the work they do and the company they work for (Achievement); do want to be treated fairly (Equity); and do want to work harmoniously and productively with others (Camaraderie). When these goals are frustrated, the company pays the price in an indifferent workforce and generally mediocre performance. There are very few individuals to whom these principles do not apply.[3]

Yes, you can learn from research, but get to know—*really know*—your employees. Ask them what motivates them. Marcus Buckingham and Curt Coffman, in *First, Break All the Rules*, tell us that great managers "recognize that each person is motivated differently, that each person has his own way of thinking and his own style of relating to others.... They tray to help each person become more and more of who he already is.[4]

So model yourself after those great managers. Remember: It's all about the people.

Appendix
Additional
Resources

NOTE

All forms included in this appendix are *samples* only. In light of changing legal requirements and state law variations, employers should always consult with employment counsel before using them.

Preemployment Application Form

XYZ Company
Application for Employment

Position applied for: _____   Date: _____

    XYZ Company ("XYZ") considers all applicants for employment without regard to race, color, religion, sex, national origin, age, disability, or status as a Covered Veteran in accordance with federal law. In addition, XYZ complies with applicable state and local laws prohibiting discrimination in employment in every jurisdiction in which it maintains facilities. XYZ also provides reasonable accommodation to individuals with a disability in accordance with applicable laws.

_____

Name   Social Security Number

_____

Current Address   City   State   ZIP Code

_____

Apartment No.   Telephone Number

 Referred by:

    Have you ever used any other name we should know in order to verify the information you provide on this Application?

☐ Yes   ☐ No   If yes, please provide other name.

_____

Are you over age 18? ☐ Yes ☐ No If not, state your age _____

If under 18, do you have a work permit? ☐ Yes ☐ No

Do you want to work ☐ Full Time ☐ Part Time
If part time, specify days and hours:

_____

Are you willing to work overtime as necessary?
☐ Yes ☐ No

Date you can start: _____   Salary desired: _____

How did you hear about the position for which you are applying? _____

Have you ever been employed by us? ☐ Yes ☐ No
If yes, when? _____
At what location? _____
Do you have any commitments to a current or former employer that might affect your employment with us (including, but not limited to, a non-competition agreement)?
☐ Yes   ☐ No   If yes, please explain:

_____

Have you ever been convicted of a crime (including convictions following a plea of guilty or no contest) in the last 10 years? Do not include minor traffic violations or convictions that have been expunged from your record.
☐ Yes   ☐ No

If yes, state nature, date, and location of conviction and any sentence imposed (jail term, probation, and so on):

If hired, can you provide proof that you are eligible to work in the United States for the company? ☐ Yes ☐ No

If no, explain your current status and eligibility for a work visa:

_____

_____

State the name of any relative in our employ:

_____

Record of Education

School	Name and Address of School	Course of Study	Number of Years Completed	Did You Graduate?	Diploma and Degree Received

Military Service Record

Have you ever served in the U.S. Armed Forces?
☐ Yes ☐ No

List duties in the Service, including special training, that are relevant to the position for which you have applied:

Skills (that you believe are related to the job for which you are applying)

Software packages with which you are familiar:

Typing _____ w.p.m. Other office equipment: _____

Are there any other experiences, skills, or abilities that you feel especially qualify you for work with our company?

Prior Work History

(List in order with current or last employer first.) Account for your employment history throughout the last 10 years and for any gaps in your employment during that time. You must complete this even if you attach a resume. If you do not want XYZ to contact one of your previous supervisors for a reference, please indicate below.

Dates From/To	Name, Address, and Telephone Number of Employer	Rate of Pay Start/Finish	Supervisor Name/Title	Reason for Leaving

Describe in detail the work you performed:

What did you like most about this job? What did you like least?

Dates From/To	Name, Address, and Telephone Number of Employer	Rate of Pay Start/Finish	Supervisor Name/Title	Reason for Leaving

Describe in detail the work you performed:

What did you like most about this job? What did you like least?

Dates From/To	Name, Address, and Telephone Number of Employer	Rate of Pay Start/Finish	Supervisor Name/Title	Reason for Leaving

Describe in detail the work you performed:

What did you like most about this job? What did you like least?

Have you ever been discharged, or resigned in lieu of discharge?

☐ Yes　　　☐ No

If yes, please explain:

Personal references (excluding relatives)

Name and Occupation	Dates Known	Address	Telephone Number
1.			
2.			
3.			

PREEMPLOYMENT STATEMENT (PLEASE READ VERY CAREFULLY, INITIAL EACH PARAGRAPH, AND SIGN BELOW)

I understand and voluntarily agree that:

_____ The information that I have provided on this application is true and complete to the best of my knowledge. Any misrepresentation or omission of any material fact in my application, resume, or any other materials, or during any interviews, will be grounds for refusal of employment, or, if I am employed, immediate termination from XYZ's employ.

_____ Any offer of employment I may receive from XYZ is contingent upon my successful completion of the Company's total preemployment screening process, including XYZ's receipt of references that it considers satisfactory.

_____ In processing my application for employment, and, if I am employed, for other employment purposes, XYZ hereby is authorized to verify all the information provided by me, and to procure or have prepared a consumer report or an investigative consumer report for this purpose concerning, among other things, my prior employment or military record, education, character, general reputation, personal characteristics, criminal record, and mode of living. I have received a separate document confirming that XYZ may obtain such a report or reports.

_____ I authorize all of my present and former employers, educational institutions, and those individuals I have listed as personal references to furnish information about my employment record, including a statement of the reason for the termination of my employment, work performance, abilities, academic record, and other qualities pertinent to my qualifications for employment, and I hereby release them from any and all liability for damages arising from furnishing the requested information.

_____ I understand that, if I am employed, I will have access to confidential information of XYZ and others, and will be legally obliged to maintain that information in strict confidence. My failure to do so would be grounds for immediate dismissal.

_____ I understand and agree that if I am employed, I will comply with XYZ's policies, rules, regulations, and procedures. I also understand that my employment and compensation can be terminated with or without cause or prior notice at any time, at the option of either XYZ or me. I further understand that no manager or other representative of XYZ other than the president has any authority to enter into any agreement with me for employment for any specified period of time or to make any agreement different from or contrary to any XYZ policy. I further understand that any such agreement, if made, shall not be enforceable unless it is in writing and signed by me and by the president.

Signature _____ Date_____

---

*NOTE: UNDER MARYLAND LAW, AN EMPLOYER MAY NOT REQUIRE OR DEMAND, AS A CONDITION OF EMPLOYMENT, PROSPECTIVE EMPLOYMENT, OR CONTINUED EMPLOYMENT, THAT AN INDIVIDUAL SUBMIT TO OR TAKE A LIE DETECTOR OR SIMILAR TEST. ANY EMPLOYER WHO VIOLATES THIS LAW IS GUILTY OF A MISDEMEANOR AND SUBJECT TO A FINE NOT EXCEEDING $100.

Acknowledged: Date: _____

Applicant Signature

Offer Letter

Dear _____:

This letter confirms your discussion regarding employment by XYZ Company as [Position Title] in the [Name of Department] effective [date]. Your initial salary will be at the biweekly rate of $_____ ($_____ if annualized). There will be a six-month initial evaluation of your performance.

If these terms reflect your understanding of the discussion, please sign both copies, retaining one for your files and returning the other to the Human Resources Department [or manager] no later than [date]. If your understanding is different from the above, please contact me immediately.

Enclosed is your orientation schedule. You will meet with various XYZ Company staff to discuss payroll procedures and XYZ Company and departmental policies and procedures. Please take a moment to review the Immigration Reform and Control Act information enclosed and bring the necessary documents with you on your first day. The Immigration and Naturalization Service requires you to present the documents necessary for us to complete our paperwork within three business days of your employment. **Your position offer is contingent on your ability to produce the necessary documents within the three-day period.**

This offer letter and any other XYZ Company documents are not contracts of employment, meaning that any individual who is hired may voluntarily leave employment upon proper notice, and may be terminated at any time and for any reason.

We are pleased that you have decided to join our staff, and we are sure that you will enjoy your association with XYZ Company.

Sincerely,

Jane Smith

director, human resources

Understood and agreed:

_____

John Smith

Position Description Questionnaire

Section 1
Name of supervisor completing this questionnaire:

Direct phone number:

E-mail:

Title:

Department:

Today's date:

Title of job being reviewed:

Current grade of this job:

Name of employee (s) currently in this job:

Section 2
1. List the major duties of the job (the specific tasks the employee performs):
- ✓
- ✓
- ✓
- ✓
- ✓
- ✓
- ✓

2.   Besides the education and experience requirements, are there any other special qualifications or skills that are necessary for this job?

Section 3: Job Factors: This section must be completed for all jobs.

Title of Job Under Review_____
Supervisor: _____

Directions: For each factor, check the **one box** that most closely applies to the job under review.

1. EXPERIENCE

The level of prior experience <u>required</u> to meet minimum standards of effective job performance. These are the standards without which a candidate **would not be considered for the job.** Please note that we are asking **what the job requires**, not what the current employee may actually have in terms of experience.

Check one box	Definition
	No experience necessary
	Less than one year
	One year but less than three years
	Three years but less than five years
	Five years or more

2. EDUCATION

Minimum education necessary to meet requirements of the job. This is the education level without which a candidate **would not be considered for the job**. Please note that we are asking **what the job requires**, not what the current employee may actually have in terms of education.

Check one box	Definition
	High school diploma or equivalent
	High school or four-year technical school plus: ✓ two years formal training in a technical specialty or ✓ two years of college or ✓ comparable education
	Bachelor's degree or comparable education
	Master's degree or bachelor's degree plus additional training in a specialty resulting in certification or the equivalent.
	Doctorate degree or the equivalent

3. PHYSICAL DEMANDS

Check one box	Definition
	Very light physical effort. Typical of most office jobs. Work in comfortable positions.
	Appreciable physical effort or strain. Moderately heavy lifting, pulling, and pushing activity. May include reaching, constant stooping, or standing.
	Strenuous or continuous physical effort

4. WORKING CONDITIONS/TRAVEL

Degree to which job requires working under relatively unpleasant conditions, such as noise, changing temperature, odors, monotony, frequent travel, and so on.

Check one box	Definition
	Normal light, heat, air, and space in work environment. Little or no travel—once or twice a year at most.
	Occassional exposure to one or more mildly unpleasant conditions OR Some scheduled travel three to five times a year.
	Intermittent exposure to one or more unpleasant physical conditions OR Occasional travel required, usually scheduled, six to nine times a year.
	Continuous exposure to several disagreeable physical conditions OR Travel required, 10 to 12 times a year; occassionally unscheduled.
	Continuous exposure to extremely difficult or disagreeable physical conditions OR Extensive travel required, 12 times or more per year, often unscheduled.

5. MENTAL DEMANDS

Complexity and variety of decisions that must be made; speed and accuracy required in making these decisions; amount of mental effort and independent thinking required to anticipate, plan, and solve problems arising on the job. This factor measures the degree of initiative, resourcefulness, and ingenuity required.

Check one box	Definition
	Variety of fairly routine work using standard operating procedures and needing mostly repetitive decisions. Work involves mental and visual attention, reasonable accuracy, and some pressure.
	Job involves variety of problems to be solved using general guidelines and calls for a limited number of types and decisions, some of which are complex, but most of which are subject to check. Unusual problems are referred to a supervisor.
	Job involves a variety of complex problems on matters of significance to organization, many of which, however, can be anticipated or are recurring in nature. Considerable latitude and independence in operation; only some decisions are subject to check. Fairly constant concentration required. Solutions to problems often require coordination with other departments.
	Job involves a variety of complex, changing problems on matters of significance to organization, many of which cannot be anticipated or solved by applying standard procedures or precedents. Requires careful analysis on the effect on other activities. Works under considerable pressure. Involved are high degrees of conceptual ingenuity and initiative.

6. CONSTITUENCY

This category measures scope, reason for, and complexity of interactions with various clients or audiences of the organization.

Check one box	Definition
	Provides information to other organization employees, members of the public, and organization members.
	Investigates, interprets, or advises other organization employees, members of the public, and organization members.
	Persuades or educates various audiences and attempts to influence course of action, policies, plans, and so on, of various audiences including government officials.
	Authorizes, arbitrates, and/or determines courses of action, policies, plans, and so on, including high-ranking government officials or organization members, members of Congress, members of the board of directors, and so on.

7. DEGREE OF AUTONOMY

Degree to which supervisor needs to directly oversee this position and the frequency of checks needed for this work.

Check one box	Definition
	Immediate supervision: instructions on how to do the work and are specific and detailed; work is checked often and upon completion.
	General supervision: instructions on how to do the work are outlined or explained in general terms; work is reviewed at regular intervals and upon completion.
	General direction: methods of performing tasks are left mostly to the judgement of the employee with occassional instructions given by the supervisor; work is reviewed occassionally for general effectiveness.
	Independent: methods of performing tasks are the full responsibility of the employee who has wide latitude in interpreting and applying policies and regulations; performance is measured by total results to the organization.

8. SUPERVISORY RESPONSIBILITY

Number of people—external contractors as well as internal staff—supervised. Also considered, however, is the nature of the group supervised and complexity of the function. This factor measures the extent to which the employee is required to guide, supervise, instruct, assist, or assign work to others.

Check one box	Definition
	Exercises no supervision or instruction of other employees.
	Occassionally instructs and assists other employees or makes work assignments to others as directed by a supervisor, or directly supervises one employee.
	Supervises at least two full-time employees and performs typical supervisory actions, such as writing and conducting performance evaluations.
	Supervising at least one other supervisor.
	Has authority and responsibility for personnel actions in multiple program areas.

9. FISCAL RESPONSIBILITY

The time, care, and attention to fiscal matters required of the employee. This factor gives credit for obligation to conserve such tangible assets of the association as its buildings, equipment, supplies, investments, and cash.

Check one box	Definition
	Must take reasonable care of ORGANIZA-TION property, equipment, and other assets, but cannot approve expenditures.
	Can authorize some expenditures—for example, office supplies—under $500.
	Develops and administers budget(s) for one or more units.
	Has major responsibility for financial management and overall ORGANIZATION budget.

10. IMPACT OF ERROR

This category measures the potential impact, consequences of impact, or risk to the organization if errors occur.

Check one box	Definition
	Minimal impact. Errors may result in inconvenience or minor waste, but typically would be identified by immediate supervisor within a short period of time.
	Modest impact. Errors in fact or judgement could result in modest financial losses or could undermine relationships with various audiences/clients. Within a short time frame, a supervisor could correct errors.
	Significant impact. Errors could result in financial penalties, losses, or programmatic repercussions to the organization. Errors may be undetected for several months.
	Severe impact. Errors could result in significant financial losses, lawsuits, serious damage to relationships with partners, and other audiences. Errors may go undetected for a significant amount of time.

Sample Job Description

Job descriptions serve as a useful management tool for understanding the role of the support staff, the hiring and placing of applicants, establishing salary structure, and for setting guidelines for promotions and transfers.

Office Manager/Executive Assistant

Position Summary:

The Office Manager/Executive Assistant is responsible for the sound management of all day-to-day operational functions. Provides administrative and secretarial support to the president. Develops and administers human resources and coordinates with controller. Oversees administration programs and processes designed to attract, retain, and motivate employees. Plans and carries out policies relating to all phases of human resources and administration activities.

The work involves a broad range of related activities that the Office Manager/Executive Assistant must direct and manage in terms of the stated scope and specification of all office activity. The Office Manager/Executive Assistant is expected to exercise considerable independent judgment and decision-making to resolve unusual or complex matters in a manner that is consistent with the preference of the president. The incumbent reports to and may seek direction from the president, but maintains full and direct accountability for final results. The incumbent regularly communicates with the president and coordinates with him on planning.

Essential Functions:
- ✓ Analyzes and organizes office operations and procedures.
- ✓ Implements day-to-day human resources matters including: recruiting, orientation, training, performance evaluation, attendance, and benefits administration.

✓ Maximizes office productivity through proficient use of appropriate software applications.

✓ Formulates procedures for systematic retention, protection, retrieval, transfer, and disposal of records.

✓ Types correspondence for the president, including handling of confidential information.

✓ Provides administrative support for the president to include telephone coverage, mail, and necessary communications internally and externally.

✓ Assists the president in the management of his schedule.

✓ Plans office layout.

✓ Maintains personnel records to ensure completeness, accuracy, and timeliness.

✓ Coordinates activities of various workers within department.

✓ Maintains contact with employees and outside vendors. Serves as administrative liaison.

✓ Investigates employee concerns.

✓ Manages all activities related to the maintenance of the facilities, office equipment, and systems.

✓ Performs special projects as assigned by the president.

Required Experience and Training:

The position requires 10-plus years of general office management experience or any equivalent combination of experience and training that provides the required knowledge, skills, and abilities.

Knowledge and Skill Requirements:

✓ Advanced knowledge of practices, processes, and principles of office management.

✓ Knowledge of all standard operating procedures, policies, and procedures.

✓ Technologically competent, including working knowledge of Windows, Word, Excel, Outlook, and QuickBooks.

✓ Skill and ability to manage multiple/parallel projects.

✓ Skill and ability to take initiative and work under extreme pressures.

✓ Skill and ability to effectively organize/prioritize work and manage time in order to meet deadlines.

✓ Skill and ability to analyze and solve complex problems.

✓ Skill and ability to effectively communicate orally and in writing. Ability to respond to common inquiries or complaints.

✓ Skill and ability to interact with employees, external customers, contractors, subcontractors, third-party consultants, and vendors in an effective and professional manner. Ability to deliver superior customer service. Ability to establish harmonious and effective working relationships. Discreet and diplomatic.

✓ Demonstrated success in the leading and managing of people.

✓ Ability to interface well with all departments of the company and to represent the president in a highly professional manner.

✓ Ability to maintain the highest level of confidentiality.

Special Working Conditions:

This position may require extended periods of standing, sitting, as well as some repetitive movements and repetitive lifting of minimal weight.

Reasonable accommodations may be made to enable individuals with disabilities to perform the essential functions.

Employee File Checklist

_____ Employment Application/Resume

_____ Offer/Confirmation Letter

_____ Personnel Data Form/Emergency Contact Information

_____ New Hire Form

_____ Tax Forms

_____ Employee Photograph

_____ Acknowledgement Form, Receipt of Employee Handbook

_____ Acknowledgement Form, Electronic Mail, and Internet Access Policy

_____ Time and Attendance Policy

_____ Employee Change Notices

_____ Performance Evaluations

_____ Supervisor's Reports, Other Disciplinary Notices

_____ Leave of Absence Request

_____ Employment Termination Notice/Resignation Letter

_____ Exit Interview

New Employee Questionnaire

Congratulations on completing three months of employment with us. Now that you have become acquainted with the organization, please complete this questionnaire and return it to your manager. Your responses are very important to us. You are not required to sign your name, but listing your department will be helpful.

1. Was the position you applied for clearly explained during the interview process?

2. How would you rate the on-the-job training your received?

3. How would you rate the orientation?

4. How would you rate the responsiveness of other departments?

5. How would you rate the communication in your department?

6. How are the general working conditions in your department?

7. Is your position what you expected it to be?

_____

Employee Name/Date/Department

Leave of Absence Form

A. To be completed by the employee

Employee Name   Home Phone No.

_____   _____

Employee Address

_____
                    City   State   Zip Code

Department   Job Title

_____   _____

Reason for Leave of Absence

☐ Medical*   ☐ Childcare   ☐ Family Healthcare*
*Medical Certification Required

Explanation

_____

Start date of leave_____   Anticipated Return_____

Intermittent leave: _____

Dates of intended leave and intended duration:_____

Employee Signature

_____
                                          Date

 B. To be completed by human resources

Medical Certification Received (if applicable):

 Yes ☐ No ☐ FMLA Leave

Comments:

Leave Approved	Leave Denied
Supervisor Date	Supervisor Date
Second-Level Management Date	Second-Level Management Date
Human Resource Manager Date	Human Resource Manager Date

New Employee 3-Month Evaluation

Employee   Position

_____   _____

Department   Start Date

_____   _____

Initial Review Period Ends   Reviewer

_____   _____

ABILITY TO LEARN/JOB KNOWLEDGE: Has the employee made appropriate progress in understanding the responsibilities/goals of the new position?

QUALITY/QUANTITY OF WORK: Is employee's volume, accuracy, and quality of work appropriate to current length of experience in this position?

RESPONSIBILITY/DEPENDABILITY: Does employee fulfill responsibilities to extent expected? Has attendance been satisfactory? Is employee punctual?

Required Questions:

1. Is the employee performing to the expectation of the supervisor?

2. Is the employee a team player?

_____

3. Are there any problem areas?

_____

4. Does the employee have any concerns?

_____

Other comments regarding present performance:

Action:

_____Progress is completely satisfactory. Employment is confirmed.

_____Progress is generally adequate; more time is required. Initial review period is extended through _____. Performance will be reassessed at that time.

_____Progress is less than adequate. There has been a conversation (with a plan of action) and memo to file prepared. Performance will be reassessed on _____.

Reviewer's Signature/Date_____

Employee's Signature/Date_____

Our company is interested in your opinions and comments. Your work performance has been evaluated by your supervisor and you are invited to record your comments

Sample Performance Appraisal Form

(Please note: Performance appraisal forms should be designed to further the goals and reflect the culture of your organization, and should be tailored to meet the key functions of the employee being reviewed (for example, sales vs. administrative staff, non-supervisory vs. supervisory).

A Performance Appraisal is designed to accomplish the following objectives:

✓ Direct efforts toward achievement of our company goals.

✓ Enhance employee performance.

✓ Foster ongoing effective communications between managers and employees.

✓ Provide an opportunity for employee's professional growth.

Objectives

At the beginning of the evaluation cycle, the manger and the employee agree on the work to be done and decide how the results will be measured. They should also reach agreement on weights.

Performance factors

Next, the manager and the employee will review the performance factors and determine on which ones to focus during the period. This is a good opportunity for both parties to discuss the behaviors that will support each selected performance factor.

Development plan

Also identify development plans at the beginning of the review period. Include ways to improve performance on the present job and ways to develop new skills for the future.

Employee Identification Information			
Employee:		Supervisor:	
Job Title:		Reviewer:	
Department:			
Period Covered From:			
Mid-Year Completion Date:			

Check one:			
	Mid-Year Close-Out		Year End

Section I: Objectives		
OBJECTIVES	RESULTS (describe work performance)	RATING

Section II: Performance Factors— select the ones to focus on this cycle			
Performance Factors	**"✓" If Key Factor**	**Results (describe work performance)**	**Rating**
Attendance			
Communications			
Cooperation and Teamwork			
Coordination			
Creativity			
Customer Service			
Initiative			
Interpersonal Relationships			
Job Knowledge			
Managing Time			
Performance Consistency			
Planning			
Problem-Solving			
Quality of Work			
Quantity of Work			
Timeliness			
Using Resources			

Section III: Managing/Supervising Performance Factors			
Performance Factors	**"✓" If Key Factor**	**Results (describe work performance)**	**Rating**
Budgeting			
Communications Link			
Feedback and Coaching			
Employee Development			
Leadership and Motivation			
Organization and Work Allocation			
Performance Reviews			
Setting Objectives			
Staffing			

Section IV: Overall Performance Rating				
	Below Standards	**Requires Improvement**	**Fully Successful**	**Exceeded Standards**
Choose one of the following:				

Section V: Development Plans		
Development Opportunities	**Specific Plans for Development (Including Time Frames)**	**Results**
Indentify development plans at the beginning of the review period.		

Section VI: Comments and Signatures

Employee Comments (Optional):

Signatures:			
Employees:		Date:	
Supervisor or Team Leader		Date:	
Reviewer:		Date:	

Performance Improvement Plan

CONFIDENTIAL MEMORANDUM

DATE: (Current date)

TO: (Employee)

FROM: (Manager)
            (Title)

SUBJECT: Performance Improvement Plan

On (date) we met to discuss your performance. During this meeting, I informed you that your performance rating for the annual evaluation cycle was Below Standards. I also showed you examples of where your work product didn't meet the agreed-upon standards. As indicated in your year-end evaluation, you required improvement in quantity of work, organizing and prioritizing assignments, and customer service skills, all of which are important components/performance factors in your work for our organization.

In order to help you improve your performance in the areas noted above, I developed the following Performance Improvement Plan (PIP). Your performance improvement period will begin on (date) and end on (date). I would like you to schedule an hour with me every two weeks to discuss our progress toward the milestones listed below. I would also like you to document your progress in writing so we can use this information as talking points at our bi-monthly meetings.

A Fully Successful level of performance will include the satisfactory accomplishment and demonstration of the following performance factors:

Quantity of work

Due to constant revisions because of incomplete and incorrect final reports, the lag in workflow is impeding the work of our department.

Performance Expectation:

✓ Submit draft reports to me to ensure that they are complete and error-free before finalizing.

Organizing and prioritizing assignments

Handling multiple tasks simultaneously is an important job responsibility. Finding efficient ways to manage your work can prevent important projects from slipping through the cracks. For example, when you did not follow up to clarify the time for the food delivery for our reception, it was not delivered on a timely basis, causing a disruption in our event.

Performance Expectation:

✓ Work closely with other administrative staff to explore different methods of accomplishing tasks.

✓ Seek clarity by asking questions when you are unsure of assignment specifications.

✓ Manage vendor commitments.

Customer service

Providing lead telephone reception for the department is a very visible responsibility that delivers a critical first impression of our association. Timely fulfillment of member/client requests and prompt responses to telephone inquiries have suffered greatly in the past two months. For example, members often indicated that they have not received requested items and materials from you. It is essential that you answer the phone in a prompt and courteous manner, responding to requests within 24 hours.

Performance Expectation:

✓ Answer the phone in a prompt and courteous manner, responding to requests within 24 hours.

The previous information represents the expectations that I have of you in your role here. Please know that I am available to assist you in improving your performance in the areas previously outlined.

I look forward to working with you during these next few weeks. Again, I am available to answer any questions you may have or to provide you with any guidance you may require to improve your job performance. However, you should be aware that if you do not improve your performance to a Fully Successful level by (date), or if you have not completed the outlined assignments within the specified time frames and according to the expectations given, I will consider additional measures to address continued performance concerns, which may include recommending termination of your employment. Please let me know if you have any questions or concerns.

I have read and understand this PIP, and I have had the opportunity to discuss it with my supervisor. I understand that termination is a possible consequence if I do not meet and sustain the expectations contained in this Performance Improvement Plan.

Employee's Signature   Date

Sample Warning Memorandums

CONFIDENTIAL MEMORANDUM

DATE: (Current date)

TO: (Employee)

FROM: (Manager)
          (Title)

SUBJECT: Performance Problems

The intent of this memorandum is to follow up on our conversation of [date of most recent counseling] regarding [describe performance/conduct problem(s)] _____, and to ensure that you understand [Company name]'s expectations going forward.

As you know, we have had several discussions regarding this issue, on [dates of prior discussions]. [Briefly summarize what was discussed in counseling discussions prior to most recent counseling, what has occurred since the last counseling discussion, and the negative impact of the employee's behavior. For example, in those discussions I shared with you my concern about your pattern of late arrivals to work. Despite those discussions, you have continued to arrive at work between 15–30 minutes late on average two or three times a week. Your late arrivals impose an extra burden on your coworkers and have a negative impact on the efficiency of our operations.

When we met on [date of most recent counseling], I emphasized to you that it is critical that you _____ [make performance/conduct expectations clear; for example, arrive to work at your scheduled start time unless you have received prior authorization from your supervisor to arrive at a later time]. If you fail to meet this requirement, you will be subject to serious disciplinary consequences, up to and including termination of your employment with [Company name].

[Employee's first name], I'd like very much to help you succeed on your job here, and I hope that you are able to meet these expectations of your job. If you have any suggestions for how I can help you to improve in this area, I would be happy to discuss them with you.

I would also like to remind you of the resources that are available to you as a [Company name] employee. [List contact info that might be relevant given nature of employee's performance/conduct issues, Employee Assistance Program, Human Resources Department, and so on.]

I have read this warning and have had the opportunity to discuss it with my manager. I understand that my failure to comply with the expectations it contains will be grounds for serious disciplinary action, up to and including termination of my employment.

_____

Manager's Signature   Date

_____

Employee's Signature   Date

Sample Memorandum of Final Warning

CONFIDENTIAL MEMORANDUM

DATE: (Current date)
TO: (Employee)
FROM: (Manager)
                (Title)
SUBJECT: Performance Problems—Final Warning

The intent of this memorandum is to follow up on our conversation of [date] regarding _____,
and to confirm that this discussion was a final warning.

As you know, we have had previous discussions regarding this issue. [Briefly summarize what was discussed, and when.] You also have received (a) written warning(s) about your unsatisfactory [performance/conduct].

Despite those efforts to move your [performance/conduct] back on track, you continue to [describe employee's continuing problems]. It is critical that _____ [make expectations clear].

Please understand that this is a final warning. Any further unsatisfactory conduct or job performance on your part will result in your immediate dismissal.

I have read this final warning and have had the opportunity to discuss it with my manager. I understand that further unsatisfactory conduct or job performance on my part will result in my immediate termination.

_____
Supervisor's Signature   Date

_____
Employee's Signature   Date

Internal Investigation Outline

Internal Investigation Outline
Developed by Taren McCombs, HR Executive, SPHR

Section One: Background
(Briefly describe the facts giving rise to the investigation.)

For example: We understand from your supervisor that you have complained about certain behaviors that one of your colleagues have directed toward you. We also understand that you believe these behaviors may constitute sexual harassment. Because the company views these matters very seriously, we are compelled to conduct an internal investigation—beginning with this interview.

Section Two: Investigation Protocol
(Review the following with each person interviewed.)

1. Interviewer's role: We are conducting this interview to provide you with an opportunity to respond to information provided to Human Resources as a result of the complaint we received. The information that you provide us today may help us determine the appropriate course of action.

2. Confidentiality: We are committed to conducting a fair and objective investigation. Therefore, we will not draw any conclusions or make any recommendations until after we have obtained your responses.

We will only share the information that we obtain from you with those that have a legitimate business need to know.

(*For the complaining employee only:* You should be aware, however, that it may be necessary to discuss the information that you share with us with the accused and others, as appropriate and at the appropriate time.)

3. <u>Retaliation</u>: The company will not tolerate retaliation or reprisals against anyone who shares knowledge or information during this investigation.

4. <u>Factual Responses</u>: You should be aware that anyone who intentionally provides false information or misdirects this investigation will be subject to disciplinary action, up to and including termination of employment. Accordingly, we will depend upon your open and honest responses to the questions that we ask today.

Section Three: <u>Interview Questions</u>

(Insert non-leading questions designed to clarify the issues in dispute. Provide interviewee with an opportunity to respond to all questions/allegations. Develop different questions for the complaining employee, alleged offender, and witnesses. <u>Do not</u> ask interviewees to draw conclusions. Seek facts only.)

Sample questions for a sexual harassment investigation:

1. What happened?
2. When did it happen?
3. Who is the alleged harasser?
4. When and where did the incident(s) take place?
5. Where there any witnesses to the incidents?
6. Where the incidents isolated or part of a continuing practice?
7. What was the reaction of the complaining employee?
8. How has the incident(s) affected the complaining employee personally and in the ability to perform work?
9. Has the complaining employee discussed the matter with anyone else?
10. Is there any documentation related to the incidents (for example, e-mails, letters, voice mail)?

Closing Question: To help us ensure a fair and objective investigation into this matter is there anything else that you would like to tell us?

Section Four: <u>Closing Comments</u>

1. *Review notes for accuracy* and obtain the employee's signature and date below.

2. *Reinforce Confidentiality:* Again, we will limit the disclosure of this information to those who have a legitimate business need to know. Likewise, we ask that you keep this information confidential and that you do not discuss this matter with anyone.

3. *Follow Up:* We may need to follow up with you during the investigation and your continued cooperation may be necessary to help reach a resolution. Please feel free to contact me should you remember any additional information or if new information becomes available.

4. *Next Steps:* We will continue to speak with others as necessary to reach a fair determination regarding next steps. Once we make a determination and share recommendations with (insert title of appropriate party), we will advise you of the outcome of the investigation.

I have had the opportunity to confirm my responses to the above questions and the contents accurately reflect my conversation with (Insert interviewer's name).

_____   _____

Signature (Interviewee)   *Date*

Exit Interview Form

Companies often conduct interviews with exiting employees in order to understand the real reasons employees leave and to obtain information on processes, people, and departments that might need some redirection. If this valuable information is analyzed and necessary changes are made, employee turnover can be reduced.

Here are some sample questions you might consider:

- ✓ Why are you leaving?
- ✓ What did you like most about your job?
- ✓ If you could improve the job in any way, what would you suggest?
- ✓ How did you feel about the general working conditions at X?
- ✓ Did you think your pay was fair?
- ✓ What did you think of the benefits?
- ✓ Are there any benefits that you feel we should be offering that we currently are not?
- ✓ How would you describe the morale in your workgroup?
- ✓ How would you describe the morale at X in general?

Using the scale of Excellent/Good/Fair/Poor, how would you rate the following items relative to your job?

- ✓ Cooperation within your workgroup.
- ✓ Cooperation from other workgroups.
- ✓ Communication within your workgroup.
- ✓ Communication with other workgroups.
- ✓ Opportunity for advancement.

Using the scale of Excellent/Good/Fair/Poor, how would you rate the following items relative to your supervisor?

- ✓ Providing you with necessary information to perform your job efficiently and effectively?
- ✓ Providing you with necessary training.
- ✓ Providing you with recognition on the job.
- ✓ Assisting with your career development.
- ✓ Creating an environment of cooperation and team-work.
- ✓ Providing you with frequent coaching and balanced feedback.
- ✓ Encouraging and listening to your suggestions.
- ✓ Resolving complaints and problems effectively.
- ✓ Following policies and procedures.

Would you recommend that a friend or acquaintance apply for a job here? Why or why not?

If you could change three things about your department and three things about the company, what would they be?

Where are you going to work?

What will your job responsibilities be?

What appears better to you in your new position compared to your position with us?

Additional comments?

Federal Labor Laws by Number of Employees

1–14 Employees
- ✓ Fair Labor Standards Act (FLSA) (1938).
- ✓ Immigration Reform & Controls Act (IRCA) (1986).
- ✓ Employee Polygraph Protection Act (1988).
- ✓ Uniformed Services Employment & Re-employment Rights Act of 1994.
- ✓ Equal Pay Act of 1963.
- ✓ Consumer Credit Protection Act of 1968.
- ✓ National Labor Relations Act (NLRA) (1935).
- ✓ Labor-Management Relations Act (Taft-Hartley) (1947).
- ✓ Employee Retirement Income Security Act (ERISA) 1974) (if company offers benefits).
- ✓ Uniform Guidelines of Employee Selection Procedures (1978).
- ✓ Federal Insurance Contributions Act of 1935 (FICA) (Social Security).

11–19, add
- ✓ Occupational Safety & Health Act (OSHA) (1970).

15–19, add
- ✓ Civil Rights Act of 1964 Title VII, Civil Rights Act of 1991.
- ✓ Title I, Americans with Disabilities Act of 1990 (ADA).

20–49, add
- ✓ Age Discrimination in Employment Act (1967) (ADEA).

✓ Consolidated Omnibus Budget Reconciliation Act of 1985 (COBRA).

50 or more, add
✓ Family and Medical Leave Act of 1993 (FMLA).
✓ EEO-1 Report filed annually w/EEOC if organization is a federal contractor.

100 or more, add
✓ Worker Adjustment and Retraining Notification Act of 1989 (WARN).
✓ EEO-1 Report filed annually w/EEOC if organization is not a federal contractor.

Federal Contractors, add
✓ Executive Orders 11246 (1965), 11375 (1967), 11478 (1969).
✓ Vocational Rehabilitation Act of 1973.
✓ Drug Free Workplace Act of 1988.
✓ Vietnam-Era Veterans Readjustment Act of 1974.
✓ Davis Bacon Act of 1931.
✓ Copeland Act of 1934.
✓ Walsh-Healy Act of 1936.

Federal and State Posting Requirements

FEDERAL Posting Requirements

Many federal employment laws require employers to post notices informing employees of their rights in areas of the workplace that are conspicuous and accessible to all employees. The U.S. Department of Labor publishes a Poster Advisor *(www.dol.gov/elaws/posters.htm)*. The Poster Advisor is designed to help employers comply with the poster requirements of several laws administered by the U.S. Department of Labor (DOL). These laws require employers to display official DOL posters where employees can readily observe them. DOL provides the posters at no cost to employers. The Poster Advisor only provides information about Federal DOL poster requirements.

New Minimum Wage Posters Available on DOL Site
www.shrm.org/government/update/071307_4.asp

New Federal Minimum Wage Poster *www.dol.gov/esa/ regs/compliance/posters/pdf/minwagebw.pdf—English*

www.dol.gov/esa/regs/compliance/posters/flsaspan.htm — Spanish

www.dol.gov/esa/regs/compliance/posters/pdf/ minwagecn.pdf—Chinese

STATE Posting Requirements

Most states have also enacted provisions requiring employers to post certain notices within their workplaces. You will find all states' DOL posting requirements on SHRM's site *www.shrm.org/ hrresources/stresources/workplacepost.asp*. If a particular state does not appear on the chart, it is due to our not finding any evidence a statute exists for that state.

New OSHA Poster

The OSHA poster, also known as the OSHA notice of employee rights, is required to be displayed in every workplace in America. The poster informs employers and employees of their rights and responsibilities for a safe and healthful workplace.

Additional resources

Associations

American Society for Training and Development—leading association for workplace learning and performance professionals. (*www.astd.org*)

Human Resource Planning Society—global association of senior HR professionals in the world's leading organizations. (*www.hrps.org*)

Society for Human Resource Management—serves the needs of the human resource management professional by providing the most essential and comprehensive set of resources available. In addition, the Society is committed to advancing the human resource profession and the capabilities of all human resource professionals to ensure that HR is an essential and effective partner in developing and executing organizational strategy. (*www.shrm.org*)

WorldatWork—non-profit association dedicated to knowledge leadership in compensation, benefits and total rewards. (*www.worldatwork.org*)

Websites

About.com HR
Information, forms, new articles on timely HR topics
www.humanresources.about.com

About.com Management
Information, forms, new articles on timely management topics
www.management.about.com

HR.com
Place to network with HR professionals
www.hr.com

hrVillage

Free info and connections with vendors and providers

www.hrVillage.com

Department of Labor Wage and Hour Division

www.dol.gov/esa/whd/

Fair Labor Standards Act

www.dol.gov/esa/whd/flsa/

Management Library

A complete integrated online free management library for nonprofits and for-profits.

www.managementhelp.org/

Occupational Safety and Health Administration

www.osha.gov

Small Business Administration

www.osha.gov

Glossary

Affirmative action—any program, policy, or procedure an employer implements to correct past discrimination and prevent current and future discrimination in the workplace.

Affirmative action plan—a written affirmative action program that must be adopted pursuant to Executive Order 11246 by any non-construction contractor with 50 or more employees and federal government contracts of $50,000 or more.

Age Discrimination in Employment Act of 1967 (ADEA)—a federal law applicable to employers of 20 or more employees, prohibiting discrimination based on age against employees or job applicants age 40 or older (with no upper age limit) in favor of a younger person.

Americans with Disabilities Act of 1990 (ADA)—a federal law applicable to employers of 15 or more that bars discrimination against employees or job applicants because of their physical or mental disability; it requires the employer to provide reasonable accommodations to disabled individuals during both the hiring process and employment.

Baby Boomers—the generation born between 1946 and 1964.

Behavioral interview—a carefully planned interview, based on the job and its outcomes, using the principle that past performance is the best indicator of future behavior. Specifically, it assumes that the way a job applicant has used his or her skills in the past will predict how he or she will use them in a new job. Interviewers should design questions to draw out candidates' stories of real-life experiences that illustrate their ability to perform the essential functions, reach the applicable goals, and excel in the job.

Benefits—employer-provided "extras" other than pay that have financial value for employees.

C-Suite—an organization's executive team, such as Chief Executive Officer (CEO), Chief Operating Officer (COO), Chief Financial Officer (CFO), and so on.

Capital expenditure—payment for the purchase, replacement, or expansion of facilities.

Career management system—a program intended to retain employees by helping them acquire and develop skills and abilities beyond those they already possess.

Career path—the progression of positions an employee moves through during his or her employment.

Chain of command—the order of positions according to responsibility and authority.

Compensation—financial payment for work performed, as in wages and salaries.

Competencies—refers to a set of knowledge, skills, and abilities needed to perform a specific job.

Consolidated Omnibus Budget Reconciliation Act of 1986 (COBRA)—a federal law granting certain former employees, retirees, spouses, ex-spouses, and dependent children the right to temporary continuation of health coverage at the pertinent organization's group rates.

Contingency planning—the process of identifying an organization's critical operating systems and how to keep them functioning in emergencies.

Corporate culture—the values, beliefs, and practices of an organization that directly influence the organization's, and its employees', conduct and behavior.

Corporate values—The most important principles of an organization; often joined with its mission statement.

Cost-per-hire—the direct and indirect costs incurred in filling a position.

Counseling—in a managerial context, supportive guidance to help an employee work through issues that affect job performance.

Crisis management—organization-wide policies and procedures for responding to events such as natural disasters, product failures, or other events that threaten an organization or its operation.

Development—teaching employees the skills needed for current and future jobs.

Direct labor—people who actually produce or provide an organization's products or services.

Disciplinary action—steps taken against an employee who fails to meet performance or behavioral standards.

Diversity—differences age, sexual orientation, race, religion, and similar categories, among a group.

Dividend—money or stock a company pays to its shareholders.

Downsizing—reducing an organization's workforce by eliminating positions.

E-commerce—paperless, electronic business transactions.

Employee handbook or manual—written information covering the employer's policies and procedures.

Employee Retirement Income Security Act of 1974 (ERISA)—a federal law setting minimum standards for pension plans in private industry.

Employee Stock Ownership Plan (ESOP)—a trust established by the employer that operates as a tax-qualified, defined-contribution retirement plan, in which the employer's contributions are invested in company stock.

Employee Stock Purchase Plan—an employer-sponsored plan that lets employees buy company stock below its fair market price.

Employee training—learning planned by the company to provide job-related knowledge, skills, abilities, and behaviors.

Employer of choice—an organization whose reputation and business practices make it such a great place to work that job applicants prefer it to another.

Employment-at-will—the employment law concept that both employers and employees can terminate the employment relationship at any time and for any lawful reason or for no reason.

Equal Employment Opportunity Commission (EEOC)—the U.S. agency that implements and enforces most federal anti-discrimination laws.

Equal Pay Act of 1963—a federal law requiring that men and women employed in the same establishment receive equal pay for work of equal effort, skill, and responsibility.

Ethics—the branch of knowledge that deals with moral principles, including correct conduct or behavior.

Exempt employees—those employees who—because of their duties and mode or level of compensation—are exempt from the minimum wage and overtime pay requirements of the federal Fair Labor Standards Act (FLSA).

Exit interview—a meeting with a departing employee regarding his or her reason for leaving an organization and other observations on the person's experience there.

External audit—assessment by an independent firm, based on generally accepted auditing procedures, to verify the accuracy of an organization's financial statements.

Fair Labor Standards Act of 1938 (FLSA)—a federal law establishing minimum wage, overtime pay, record-keeping, and child labor standards that affect full-time and part-time workers in the private sector, and in federal, state, and local governments.

Family and Medical Leave Act of 1993 (FMLA)—a federal law providing the eligible employees of covered employers up to 12 weeks of unpaid leave in any 12-month period for:

- ✓ The employee's own serious health condition.
- ✓ Taking care of a spouse, parent, or child with a serious health condition.
- ✓ The birth of a child to the employee.
- ✓ The employee's adoption or foster care of a child.

Feedback—an ongoing workplace conversation about how well an employee is performing his or her job.

Fiduciary—a person, organization, or association that stands in a special relation of trust, confidence, or responsibility and is responsible for holding assets in trust for a beneficiary.

Form 5500 Annual Report—the annual return filed with the federal Employee Benefits Security Administration to report on employee pension and welfare benefit plans.

Gap analysis—means of measuring and evaluating differences between a current position and what the organization wants it to become in the future.

Gen X—people born between 1965 and 1976.

Gen Y—people born between 1979 and 1994.

General ledger—a financial book of final entry summarizing a company's financial transactions by offsetting debit and credit transactions.

Glass ceiling—a term for the barrier that prevents women and minorities from being widely represented in top positions at work.

Globalization—the process of all countries becoming one community.

Governance—the ultimate action of management and leadership, often the function of a board of directors.

Health Insurance Portability & Accountability Act of 1996 (HIPAA)—a federal law that safeguards health insurance continuity and the privacy of certain medical data for employees who change jobs and their dependents.

Health Maintenance Organization (HMO)—a business that provides comprehensive health services for a flat fee.

Human Resource Information System (HRIS)—computer software for tracking employee and applicant information and other HR data.

Human resource management—administering the policies, practices, and systems that affect employees in the workplace.

Immigration Reform and Control Act of 1986 (IRCA)—a federal law, applicable to employers of four or more employees, making it unlawful to hire any person not legally authorized to work in the United States; requiring employers to verify the employment eligibility of all new employees; and prohibiting discrimination on the basis of national origin or citizenship against any individual in the hiring or firing process.

Job description—a written document detailing the requirements and responsibilities of a specific position.

Management—the responsibility for and control of an organization.

Merit raise—a pay increase based on good performance.

Mission statement—the written documentation of an organization's purpose.

Negligent hiring—a legal claim available in some states, based on the theory that the employer should compensate a person who has been harmed by an individual the employer hired without exercising reasonable care.

Occupational Safety and Health Act of 1970—a federal law that imposes a general duty on employers to maintain a workplace free from recognized safety or health hazards, and establishes the Occupational Safety and Health Administration (OSHA).

Offshoring—the practice of relocating business processes to other countries where labor costs are lower than in the United States.

On-the-job training—having a person learn job-related tasks by doing them.

Onboarding—the process of orienting new employees to the organization and to their new position.

Operating budget—a detailed list of all income and expenses during a specific period.

Orientation—a program designed by the company to inform new employees about its workplace, culture, policies, procedures, and benefits.

Occupational Safety and Health Administration (OSHA)—an agency within the U.S. Department of Labor that is responsible for establishing workplace safety standards and conducting inspections to ensure they are met.

Outsourcing—an employer's contracting with a third party that agrees to provide a service the employer previously provided for itself.

Overhead—costs (excluding labor) associated with operating a business, including rent, utilities, taxes, and the like.

Pay grade—a designation or ranking of the pay for a group of similar jobs.

Pay range—minimum to maximum pay for particular jobs as established by the employer. Ranges vary, depending on the job's level of authority and responsibilities and its market value.

Performance appraisal—evaluation and discussion of an employee's job performance in relation to established objectives.

Performance management—the entire process of managing employee job performance, including setting goals, providing ongoing feedback, discussing job performance, and rewarding good work.

Policy—guidelines or rules on a specific issue, internal or external.

Pregnancy Discrimination Act of 1978—a federal law that amended Title VII of the Civil Rights Act of 1964 to clarify that discrimination on the basis of pregnancy, childbirth, or a related medical condition is a form of illegal sex discrimination. It requires that affected women be treated the same, for all employment-related purposes, as other employees or applicants with similar abilities or limitations.

Professional Employer Organization (PEO)—an entity that enters into a joint-employment relationship with an employer by supplying it with employees.

Profit margin—earnings expressed as a percentage of revenues.

Profit and loss statement—a financial document summarizing company revenue and expenses during a specific period of time.

Progressive discipline—a system of employee discipline that starts with less serious forms of discipline, such as oral counseling, for minor performance or conduct problems, and proceeds through more serious forms, if needed, such as written warning, probation, or termination of employment.

Recruitment—attracting appropriate candidates for an employer's job openings.

Reduction in force (RIF)—an employee's or group of employees' involuntary separation from employment because of changing business needs such as economic pressures, lack of work, or organizational changes.

Reference check—verification of an applicant's information about his or her work experience.

Rightsizing—prioritizing jobs or positions so as to identify and eliminate unnecessary ones.

Risk management—for HR and business purposes, the use of insurance or other investment strategies to minimize the employer's exposure to liability in the event of a loss or injury.

Sarbanes Oxley Act of 2002 (SOX)—a federal law enacted to increase the accountability of corporations to their shareholders in the wake of major accounting scandals. Many of its provisions are not germane to HR, but the act's whistleblower protection and 401(k) blackout-notice provisions are of note.

Sexual harassment—a form of gender discrimination that consists of unwelcome sexual advances; requests for sexual favors; or other verbal, visual, or physical conduct of a sexual or gender-biased nature that affects an individual's employment, unreasonably interferes with an individual's work performance, or creates an intimidating, hostile, or offensive work environment.

Statement of Work—a detailed, formal statement of needs and requirements on which prospective suppliers base their bids or proposals.

Strategic planning—assembling a step-by-step "road map" needed to reach organizational goals.

Succession planning—identifying long-range staffing needs and the internal or external candidates to fill them.

Title VII of the Civil Rights Act of 1964 (Title VII)—a federal law, applicable to employers of 15 employees or more, prohibiting an employer from discriminating against employees or applicants based on race, color, gender, pregnancy, national origin, or religion.

W-2 form—the federal tax form employers give employees at the end of each calendar year, detailing total wages and withholdings.

W-4 form—the federal tax form that employees fill out and give to their employer so the organization can withhold the correct amounts of federal income tax from employees' pay.

Wage survey—a gathering of salary data from other companies to compare similar jobs in similar markets.

Workers' compensation—a state program that provides replacement income and medical expenses to employees who are injured or become ill because of their jobs, as well as financial benefits for the dependents and families of employees who die on the job.

Workforce planning—assessment of an organization's current staffing and projections to meet future needs.

Zero-based budgeting—a method of budgeting in which every expenditure must be justified with each new budget, as opposed to the traditional method, in which only increases in expenditures over the previous budget must be justified.

Bibliography

Armstrong, Sharon, and Madelyn Appelbaum. *Stress-free Performance Appraisals.* Franklin Lakes, N.J.: Career Press, 2003.

———. "Baby Boomers Envision their Retirement," An AARP Segmentation Analysis conducted by Roper Starch Worldwide, Inc. and AARP, 1999.

Buckingham, Marcus, and Curt Coffman. *First, Break All the Rules—What the World's Greatest Managers Do Differently.* New York: Simon and Shuster, 1999.

Caruth, Donald L., and Gail D. Handlogten. *Managing Compensation (And Understanding It Too).* Fairfield, Conn.: Quorum Books, 2001.

DeNisi, Angelo S. and Ricky W. Griffin. *Human Resource Management.* Boston: Houghton Mifflin, 2001.

Dessler, Gary. *Human Resource Management.* Upper Saddle River, N.J.: Prentice Hall, 2003.

Foulkes, Fred K. "The Expanding Role of the Personnel Function," quoted in John Ivancevich. *Human Resource Management.* New York: McGraw Hill, 2001.

Friedman, Dana. *Workplace Flexibility: A Guide for Companies,* Families and Work Institute Website, 2002.

Hankin, Harriet. *The New Workforce.* New York: AMACOM, 2005.

Hicks, Sabrina. "Successful Orientation Programs" in *Training and Development* (April 2000), quoted in Gary Dessler, *Human Resource Management.* Upper Saddle River, N.J.: Prentice Hall, 2003.

Ivancevich, John M. *Human Resource Management,* quoting Susan E. Jackson and Randall S. Schuler, "Understanding Human Resource Management in the Context of Organizations and Their Environments." New York: McGraw Hill, 2001.

Kovach, Kenneth A. *Strategic Human Resources Management.* Ocean City, Md.: University Press of America, 1996.

Losey, Mike. *The Future of Human Resources.* Hoboken, N.J.: John Wiley & Sons, Inc., 2005.

Lozar Glenn, Joanne. *Mentor Me: A Guide to Being Your Best Advocate in the Workplace.* Roanoke, Va.: National Business Education Association, 2003.

Luhrs, Janet. *The Simple Life Guide.* New York: Broadway Books, 2001.

———. "Making Work 'Work': New Ideas from the Winners of the Alfred P. Sloan Award for Business Excellence in Workplace Flexibility." Families and Work Institute, 2007.

———. *Market Pricing: Methods to the Madness.* Phoenix, Ariz.: WorldatWork, 2002.

Martin, Carolyn A. *Managing Generation Y: Global Citizens Born in the Late Seventies and Early Eighties.* Cambridge, Mass.: HRD Press, 2001.

Mathis, Robert L., and John H. Jackson. *Human Resources Management. (12th ed.)* New York, Cengage Publishing, 2008.

————. "Preparing for the Workplace of Tomorrow." San Francisco, Calif.: Hewitt Associates, 2004.

Redman, T., et al. "Performance Appraisal in an NHS Hospital," *Human Resource Management Journal,* 10 (2002): 48–62.

————. *Salary Budget Survey.* Phoenix, Ariz.: WorldatWork, annual.

Senge, Peter M. *The Fifth Discipline.* New York: Currency Doubleday, 1994.

Sirota, David, et al. *The Enthusiastic Employee—How Companies Profit by Giving Workers What They Want.* Upper Saddle River: N.J.: Pearson Education, Inc., 2005.

————. "New Book from Wharton Publishing Exposes as Myths 33 Beliefs About Work and Workers." Sirota Myths and Findings Report 2005: Sirota Survey Intelligence.

————. *Survey Handbook & Directory: A Guide to Finding and Using Salary Surveys.* Phoenix, Ariz.: WorldatWork, 2006.

————. *2004 HR Outsourcing Survey Report.* Richmond, Va.: SHRM, 2005.

Winfrey, E.C., *Kirkpatrick's Four Levels of Evaluation* (1999) in B. Hoffman (Ed.), *Encyclopedia of Educational Technology.* Reprinted with permission. Retrieved July 3, 2007 at *http://coe.sdsu.edu/eet/Articles/k4levels/start.htm.*

Further Reading

Armstrong, Sharon, and Madelyn Appelbaum. *Stress-free Performance Appraisals, 1st ed*. Franklin Lakes, N.J.: Career Press, 2003.

Bliss, Wendy. *Legal, Effective References: How to Give and Get Them*. Richmond, Va.: Society for Human Resource Management, 2001.

Branham, Leigh. *The 7 Hidden Reasons Employees Leave*. New York: AMACOM, 2005.

Buckingham, Marcus, and Curt Coffman. *First, Break All the Rules: What the World's Greatest Managers Do Differently*. New York: Simon and Schuster, 1999.

Buckingham, Marcus, and Donald Clifton. *Now, Discover Your Strengths*. New York: Simon and Schuster, 2001.

Burkholder, Nicholas, et al., *On Staffing—Advice and Perspectives from HR Leaders*. Hoboken, N.J.: John Wiley and Sons, Inc., 2004.

Chandler, Steve. *The Hands-Off Manager—How to Mentor People and Allow Them to Be Successful*. Franklin Lakes, N.J.: Career Press, 2007.

Collins, Jim. *Good to Great*. New York: Harper Business, 2001.

Daniels, Aubrey. *Bringing Out the Best in People*. New York: McGraw-Hill, 1993.

Davis, Brian L., et al. *The Successful Manager's Handbook—Development Suggestions for Today's Managers*. Minneapolis, Minn.: Personnel Decisions International, 1992.

Drucker, Peter F. *The Practice of Management*. New York: Harper Business, 1986.

Eppler, Mark. *Management Mess-Ups—57 Pitfalls You Can Avoid (And Stories of Those Who Didn't)*. Franklin Lakes, N.J.: Career Press, 2005.

Fournies, Ferdinand F. *Coaching*. New York: McGraw-Hill, 2000.

Kohn, Stephen E., and Vincent D. O'Connell. *Six Habits of Highly Effective Bosses*. Franklin Lakes, N.J.: Career Press, 2005.

Kouzes, James and Barry Posner. *Leadership Challenge*. San Francisco, Calif.: Jossey-Bass, 2002.

Kushel, Gerald. *Reaching the Peak Performance Zone*. New York: AMACOM, 1994.

Levering, Robert. *A Great Place to Work*. New York: Harper Collins, 1990.

McKirchey, Karen. *Powerful Performance Appraisals.* Franklin Lakes, N.J.: Career Press, 1998.

Miller, James, and Paul Brown. *The Corporate Coach: How to Build a Team of Loyal Customers and Happy Employees.* New York: Harper Business, 1994.

Nail, Thomas, and Cornelia Gamlem. *Roadmap to Success: 5 Steps to Putting Action into your Affirmative Action Program.* Va.: Gem Publication, 2004.

Pfeffer, Jeffrey, and C. O'Reilly III. *Hidden Value: How Great Companies Achieve Extraordinary Results with Ordinary People.* Boston, Mass.: Harvard Business School Press, 2000.

Sember, Brette McWhorter, and Terrence J. Sember. *The Essential Supervisor's Handbook.* Franklin Lakes, N.J.: Career Press, 2007.

Sirota, David., et al. *The Enthusiastic Employee—How Companies Profit by Giving Workers What They Want.* Trenton, N.J.: Wharton School Publishing, 2005.

Swan, William S. *How to Do a Superior Performance Appraisal.* New York: John Wiley & Sons, 1991.

Wilson, Jerry. *151 Quick Ideas to Inspire Your Staff.* Franklin Lakes, N.J.: Career Press, 2007.

Notes

Introduction

1. Ivancevich, *Human,* 6.
2. Ibid.
3. Ibid. 7, quoting Fred K. Foulkes, "The Expanding Role of the Personnel Function."
4. Dessler, *Human,* 2.
5. Interview, WRC-Radio, Washington, D.C. (Nov. 21, 2005).
6. *www.wegmans.com/about/pressRoom/ overview.asp#whatwebelieve* (last visited 11/13/07).

Chapter 3

1. Hicks, ed. *"Successful.*

Chapter 4

1. DeNisi and Griffin, *Human,* 267.
2. Glenn, *Mentor.*
3. Winfrey, *Kirkpatrick's.*
4. Senge, *The Fifth,* 3.

Chapter 5

1. Redman et al., "Performance," 62.

Chapter 6

1. "Employer."

Chapter 7

1. Sirota, et. al. "Survey."
2. Luhrs, "Market," 80.

Chapter 11

1. Losey, Messinger and Ulrich. *The Future.*

Chapter 12

1. Mathis, "Preparing," 1.
2. Armstrong and Appelbaum, "Baby," 6.
3. Hankin, *The New*.
4. Luhrs, *The Simple*.
5. Friedman, "Workplace," 3.
6. Luhrs, "Making."
7. Sirota, "2004."

Afterword

1. Kovach, *Strategic,* 1–4.
2. Sirota, Mischkind, Meltzer, *The Enthusiastic*.
3. Sirota, "New," 1, 15.
4. Buckingham and Coffman, *First,* 56.

Index

About the Authors

SHARON ARMSTRONG began her career in human resources in 1985 as a recruiter and trainer at a large Manhattan law firm, where she was promoted to a managerial role within six months. Following that position, she was director of human resources at another law firm and at three nonprofit associations in Washington, D.C.

Since launching Sharon Armstrong and Associates in 1998, she has consulted with many large corporations and small businesses. She has provided training and completed HR projects for a wide variety of clients in the profit and nonprofit sectors as well as in government.

Sharon received her BA cum laude from the University of Southern Maine and her master's degree in counseling from George Washington University. A certified Professional in Human Resources, she is a member of the national Society for Human Resource Management and its local chapter. She also serves on the Advisory Board of *Disability Leave and Absence Reporter,* published monthly by the Bureau of Business Practice.

Sharon is the coauthor of *Stress-free Performance Appraisals: Turn Your Most Painful Management Duty Into a Powerful Motivational Tool* and the tongue-in-jowl *Heeling the Canine Within: The Dog's Self-Help Companion.*

BARBARA MITCHELL has more than 25 years of experience in HR management and consulting, and is a principal and coowner of The Millennium Group International, LLC, a Washington, D.C.–based consulting firm dedicated to building organizational capacity.

Much of her career has been in senior HR positions with Marriott International, including staffing, employee relations, and employee communications. She also served in senior leadership positions with Eon Corporation and Human Genome Sciences, Inc.

A past president of the Employment Management Association, a professional emphasis group of the Society for Human Resource Management (SHRM), Barbara is also a past president of the Personnel and Industrial Relations Association (PIRA) of Los Angeles, the Leesburg/Greater Loudoun (VA) SHRM chapter, and WTPF, the Forum for HR Professionals.

She is completing a book, *Finders Keepers: A Back to Basics Approach to Attracting and Retaining the Best*, and she contributed to both *On Staffing: Advice and Perspective from HR Leaders* and *Cover Letters for Dummies*. She recently served on the Society for Human Resource Management's Special Expert Panel on Consulting and Outsourcing. Barbara is also a frequent speaker on topics related to recruitment, retention, generations at work, succession management, consulting, and human resources outsourcing.